I. IMHOTEP AS A DEMIGOD

IMHOTEP

The Vizier and Physician of

KING ZOSER

and afterwards

THE EGYPTIAN GOD

OF MEDICINE

BY

JAMIESON B. HURRY, M.A., M.D.

OXFORD UNIVERSITY PRESS

OXFORD

UNIVERSITY PRESS

Great Clarendon Street, Oxford OX2 6DP

Oxford University Press is a department of the University of Oxford.
It furthers the University's objective of excellence in research, scholarship,
and education by publishing worldwide in

Oxford New York

Athens Auckland Bangkok Bogotá Buenos Aires Calcutta
Cape Town Chennai Dar es Salaam Delhi Florence Hong Kong Istanbul
Karachi Kuala Lumpur Madrid Melbourne Mexico City Mumbai
Nairobi Paris São Paulo Singapore Taipei Tokyo Toronto Warsaw

with associated companies in Berlin Ibadan

Oxford is a registered trade mark of Oxford University Press
in the UK and in certain other countries

Published in the United States
by Oxford University Press Inc., New York

British Library Cataloguing in Publication Data
Data available
ISBN 0-19-924178-3

1 3 5 7 9 10 8 6 4 2

Printed in Great Britain
on acid-free paper by
Biddles Ltd., Guildford and King's Lynn

IN HONOUR

OF

IMHOTEP

'The first Figure of a Physician to stand out clearly
from the Mists of Antiquity.'—SIR W. OSLER.

THE PROLOGUE

THIS Monograph is consecrated to the memory of a distinguished magician-physician and sage who first appears on the stage of Egyptian history in the reign of King Zoser of the IIIrd Dynasty, and reappears at intervals on that stage during a period of over three thousand years. His record therefore extends over a large part of the history of ancient Egypt.

We shall attempt to trace the fortunes of Imhotep both during the period of his human activity and also during the subsequent periods when he was looked upon first as a demigod and finally as one of the full deities of Egypt. We shall also seek to analyse the forces which resulted in such an exceptional occurrence as the deification of an ordinary mortal, i. e. of one who had never been a king.

The subject is one which will interest various groups of readers. In the first place it will appeal to the lover of archaeology who is fascinated by the early story of our race and by every detail which throws light on its evolution. There is a glamour in the study of the earliest pages of civilization, wherever those pages have been written.

There will be a further appeal to the growing number of cultured persons who are thrilled by the story of ancient Egypt as it is gradually being unravelled. The land of the Pharaohs possesses a charm which can scarcely be rivalled by any other country and which steadily grows as its extraordinary history is better understood. Nowhere else do we meet with so ancient a civilization that can be reconstructed with an equal degree of certainty.

Lastly, our narrative makes its strongest appeal to the profession which in every country of the world devotes its life to the relief of suffering and the cure of disease. Of unique interest to that profession must be the life of Imhotep, one of the earliest of known physicians, who made so deep an impression on his fellow countrymen that his memory endured through many centuries until he was eventually raised to the rank of the Egyptian God of Medicine.

A further object of these pages is to draw attention to the claims of Imhotep to be acknowledged as the patronal deity of medicine—claims which were acknowledged by the Egyptian physicians and which are incomparably older than those possessed by his semi-mythical rival Asklepios.

The Author makes no claim to original discovery. His task has been the more modest but yet useful one of gathering together numerous threads spun by others, of weaving them into a connected canvas, on which he has drawn a portrait as true to life as is possible with the scanty details that have survived. His research is based partly on the writings of leading Egyptologists, British and foreign, partly on the examination of Egyptian antiquities in various museums in this and other countries, and partly also on two visits to Egypt which allowed the collection of first-hand evidence. The memories of happy days spent on the banks of the Nile have rendered this compilation a most enjoyable and interesting task.

In historical studies dealing with such a subject as Egyptology there is frequently, as in any other branch of knowledge in process of evolution, diversity of opinion even among experts ; further, what appears to be the truth to-day may be modified by fresh discoveries of temples, tombs, or papyri to-morrow. The wisest course, therefore, has seemed to him to include references on a

liberal scale, so that the reader may be fur-
nished with the authority on which statements
are founded.

An abstract of this Monograph was contributed
to the Fourth International Congress of the
History of Medicine which met last year in Geneva.
Since, however, the short time allotted to individual contributions forbade the submission of
more than a portion of the following study, it has
been thought well to publish the work *in extenso*.

My cordial thanks are due to various authorities
who have given facilities in connexion with illustrations.

The Director of the Musée des Antiquités
Égyptiennes at Cairo has kindly permitted the
reproduction of Figs. I and V ; the Ministry of
Public Works in Egypt the use of Col. Lyons's
photographs of Philae. The authorities of the
Wellcome Historical Medical Museum have given
facilities in regard to Fig. VII ; those of the
Staats-Museum of Berlin in regard to Fig. VI ;
those of the British Museum in regard to Figs. X
and XI ; the *Illustrated London News* in regard to
Fig. II ; Messrs. Methuen & Co. in regard to
Fig. XII ; the Egyptological Department of the
Liverpool University in regard to Fig. XVII. To

the late Dr. R. Caton, C.B.E., special thanks are due for the loan of blocks used in Figs. III, IV, and XIII–XVI.

Various friends have also given generous assistance in connexion with hieroglyphic readings and otherwise. Amongst them must be mentioned Sir E. A. Wallis Budge, Professor T. E. Peet, Miss Murray, Mr. C. J. S. Thompson, and Mr. W. R. Dawson. The latter has further been good enough to read through the proof sheets. I desire also to thank Dr. Alan H. Gardiner for his kindness in allowing the use of his new fount for the hieroglyphs included in this volume.

The story of Imhotep adds a fresh chapter to the History of Medicine which is gradually being compiled, thanks to the collaboration of workers all the world over.

J. B. H.

Westfield,
 Reading.

CONTENTS

CONTENTS

ILLUSTRATIONS

I

INTRODUCTION

IN the childhood of the world Egypt was the pioneer country as regards the evolution of medicine. To her belongs the high honour of having raised the healing art to a level far exceeding that hitherto attained. Both in diagnosis and in therapeutics astonishing progress was made. Even pathology attracted widespread interest; the Edwin Smith Papyrus suggests that dissection of the human body was systematically practised in ancient times.

The medical schools of Egypt, closely associated with her priestcraft and temples, were famous far and wide, her specialist physicians being summoned to attend royal and other personages in distant lands.[1] For a physician to have been educated in Egypt was in itself a passport to success. This high reputation is acknowledged by Homer when he says : ' In Egypt the men are more skilled in medicine than any of human kind.' [2]

Most of the ancient races of the world have found a place in their theology for one or more deities of medicine to whom were attributed miraculous powers in restoring sick and apparently

---

[1] Herodotus, ii. 84 ; iii. 1, 129. [2] *Odyssey*, iv. 227.

B

dying persons to health. Such deities were worshipped amongst the Persians, Hindus, Chinese, Babylonians, Aztecs, and Phoenicians *inter alios*; many of them had shrines which were resorted to by suffering men and women, whether afflicted mentally or physically.

The ancient Egyptians also had numerous deities to whom were attributed the invention of various arts and sciences, including medicine. Amongst those most generally referred to in this connexion are the falcon-headed sun-god Re, the wonder-working Isis with her son the sun-god Horus, Ptah, the ancient God of Memphis,[1] and the ibis-headed moon-god Thoth, the reputed author of religious and scientific works including treatises of medicine. Less important medical members of the Egyptian pantheon were Khnum with rams' horns and the lion-headed goddess Sekhmet, who were worshipped as the tutelary deities of procreation and childbirth.[2] All these deities, however, were probably mere mythical creations of the imagination and lack the fascination associated with a human personality.

[1] Ptah was the deity of healing in Memphis, just as each local deity was the creator and healer of his own people. Khnum was thus the healer at Aswan, and Sekhmet preceded Ptah, and consequently Imhotep, at Memphis.

[2] Other deities were closely associated with childbirth. Cf. Maspero, *Popular Stories of Ancient Egypt*, 1915, p. 36.

Of outstanding interest, therefore, is the famous Imhotep, who first appears on the stage of history as the vizier-physician of King Zoser (☉⌇⌇),[1] and who so impressed his fellow countrymen with his skill in healing disease that he was eventually raised first to the status of medical demigod and eventually to that of full deity of medicine.

Unfortunately we cannot trace his history from the beginning ; all that can be done is to collect and arrange such biographical details as have survived. Happily recent research allows of a more coherent account than was formerly possible.

Imhotep, the earliest physician of whom historical details have survived, lived in the reign of a famous Egyptian king named Zoser (☉⌇⌇) (Fig. II), a Pharaoh of the IIIrd Dynasty (*ca.* 2980–2900 B. C.).[2]

Unhappily we know nothing of his early history. No glimpse is allowed us of his birthplace or childhood ; there is no record of his appearance

[1] According to Manetho, King Athothis of the Ist Dynasty practised medicine and wrote anatomical books. No biographical details, however, have survived and the entire story may be legendary.

[2] Fig. II represents the life-size statue of King Zoser recently found at Sakkarah, and inscribed with his name as King of Upper and Lower Egypt. The figure wears the sacred wig covered with the Nemes head-dress.

The chronology adopted in this work is that of Professor Breasted's *History of Egypt*.

in the flesh, nor is anything told us of the steps by which he reached the highest post open to an official in Egypt.

Descended from a distinguished architect named Kanofer 𓆋𓏏𓂓 *Kꜣ-nfr*, and from a mother named Khreduonkh 𓄿𓏏𓆑 *Ḫrdw-ꜥnḫ*, Imhotep appears to have received a liberal education, so far as such was possible in those far-off days. At any rate he grew up an erudite, versatile man, a sort of Aristotelian genius, who took all knowledge for his province. He was distinguished for his vast learning as well as for some striking achievements, and in the course of ages became generally recognized as the Egyptian god of medicine. His name Imhotep 𓇋𓅓𓊵 signifies ' he who cometh in peace ',[1] a most appropriate name for a healer of the sick and one which must have brought solace and courage to many an anxious patient.

It will be convenient to divide his career into three periods and to consider in order :

I. IMHOTEP AS CONTEMPORARY OF KING ZOSER
(*ca.* 2980 B. C.)

II. IMHOTEP AS A MEDICAL DEMIGOD
(*ca.* 2850 B. C.–Reign of Mycerinus)

III. IMHOTEP AS FULL DEITY OF MEDICINE
(*ca.* 525 B. C.–Persian Period)

---

[1] For the construction and meaning of the name, cf. Appendix B.

II. KING ZOSER

II

IMHOTEP AS CONTEMPORARY OF KING ZOSER

IMHOTEP devoted his life to various activities which may be grouped as follows :

A. Grand Vizier.
B. Architect.
C. Chief Lector Priest or *Kheri-heb*.
D. Sage and Scribe.
E. Astronomer.
F. Magician-Physician.

A few details will be given under each of these headings :

A. IMHOTEP AS VIZIER

The office of vizier to the ruling Pharaoh was one of high dignity and responsibility. The occupant of the post was a sort of Joseph, whose jurisdiction extended over the various departments of state.[1] Although no specific duties of

[1] We owe to K. Sethe a valuable monograph, throwing a flood of light on the history of Imhotep and marshalling the evidence that he was actually a contemporary of King Zoser. K. Sethe, *Imhotep, der Asklepios der Aegypter : Ein vergötteter Mensch aus der Zeit des Königs Ḏoser. Untersuchungen zur Geschichte und Altertumskunde Aegyptens*, 1902, vol. ii. The author accepts Sethe's evidence as settling the question, although a few Egyptologists, e. g. G. Foucart, remain unconvinced.

the office under King Zoser [1] are on record, many details of the duties of viziers under later Egyptian kings are known, and we may fairly conclude that similar duties were carried out by Imhotep.[2]

The following list of titles in itself indicates the manifold responsibilities of the office : ' chief judge,' ' overseer of the King's records,' ' bearer of the royal seal,' ' chief of all works of the King,' ' supervisor of that which Heaven brings, the Earth creates and the Nile brings,' ' supervisor of everything in this entire land.' Amongst some of the departments of his office are mentioned the Judiciary, the Treasury, War (Army and Navy), the Interior, Agriculture, and the General Executive. A prodigy of efficiency must have been required to carry out such multifarious duties.

The name of the vizier was sometimes actually followed by the royal salutation ' Life, Prosperity, Health ', and in his judicial capacity he was regarded by the people as one who could not do wrong. Three of the greatest sages and authors of proverbial wisdom, Imhotep, Kegemni, and

---

[1] Also known as Tcheser, Doser or Tosorthros.

[2] Breasted, in his *Ancient Records of Egypt*, 1906, records many details of the duties of viziers. Cf. especially vol. i, pp. 122, 158, 212 ; vol. ii, pp. 268 ff. A famous vizier of the XVIIIth Dynasty, Rekhmirē, has left a long inscription in his tomb at Thebes detailing the duties of the vizier. Cf. Newberry, *Life of Rekhmara*, pp. 22 ff.

Ptah-hotpe, held the office of vizier in the Old Kingdom.

An interesting incident associated with Imhotep and King Zoser is recorded in what is known as the Legend of the Seven Years' Famine, which describes a period of terrible starvation caused by the failure of the Nile for seven consecutive years to reach its usual flood level and thus to irrigate the land sufficiently.[1] The result was that grain grew very scarce and almost everything needed for food came to an end.[2] The famine was attributed to the King's neglect to pay due honour and worship to the god Khnum 𓎛𓈖𓃟𓏤 who was one of the deities controlling the sources of the Nile.

The King, in his distress at the calamity which had befallen his country, turned to his counsellor Imhotep and questioned him about the birthplace

---

[1] This legend is inscribed on a granite rock on the island of Sehêl near Aswan, and dates from the Ptolemaic period, although in its earlier form it may be as old as the IIIrd Dynasty. For further details cf. Sethe, *Imhotep*, p. 11 ; Sir E. A. Budge, *The Legends of the Gods*, pp. lx, 120 (with text and translation).

Another view is that it was fabricated by priests in order to prove the generosity of the ancient Pharaohs and to enlist a similar generosity. Cf. Maspero, *The Dawn of Civilization*, 1894, p. 240.

[2] A similar seven years' famine in Egypt is recorded in Genesis xli. 54.

of the Nile and the god who ruled there. Unable to answer the King's questions at once, Imhotep requested leave of absence that he might consult the sacred books on the subject. After a brief absence he revealed to the King ' the hidden wonders, the way to which had been shown to no King for unimaginable ages '.[1] On receiving this report, King Zoser at once wrote to the Viceroy of Nubia, a nobleman called Meter, asking for his advice and assistance in abating the grievous state of affairs. ' I go back,' he wrote, ' in my mind to the days when I had an adviser, to the time of the gods, to the ibis-god (Thoth 𓅠), and to the chief *Kheri-heb* priest Imhotep, the son of Ptah 𓊪𓏏𓎛 [2] South of his Wall.' [3] He then proceeded to inquire what god or goddess presided over the Nile and could replenish his granaries with grain, so that the deity might be visited and propitiated.

Eventually, the King paid a personal visit to the temple of the god Khnum in order to make

[1] G. Steindorff, *The Religion of the Ancient Egyptians*, p. 101.

[2] The title ' son of Ptah ', here given to Imhotep, is an anachronism to be explained by the fact that this legend dates from Ptolemaic times, when the god Ptah had been assigned to Imhotep as a divine father. Sethe, *Imhotep*, p. 12.

[3] This title of Ptah ' South of his Wall ' is derived from the fact that, in one of his forms, that deity was worshipped in a temple on the south side of Memphis. E. A. Budge, *Gods of the Egyptians*, 1904, i, p. 514.

prayers and supplications before him, and to propitiate him with offerings. In response, the god Khnum appeared to the King in a dream, and promised that the Nile should rise and never fail again : ' It shall spread its water out, and cover all the land satisfactorily. Plants shall bend beneath their produce. . . . Want shall cease, and the emptiness of the granaries shall come to an end.'

In gratitude for Khnum's intervention, King Zoser made a decree, and endowed the temple of the god with lands and valuable gifts.[1] Gold, ivory, ebony, spices, precious stones and woods were all tithed so as to supply rich offerings for the temple. This is the prototype of temple endowments, which were doubtless used for the manifold wants of the god, for the maintenance of a sacerdotal staff, and for building operations.

B. IMHOTEP AS ARCHITECT

Imhotep, ' the chief of all the works of the King,' was also a notable architect, and in all probability designed for his royal master the well-

---

[1] ' By the advice of the learned Imhotep, Zoser had once presented this god Khnum with twelve tracts of land on both sides of the river, with all their revenues and taxes, in order that he should once more send a rich Nile into the country which was suffering from its seventh year of scarcity.' A. Erman, *Handbook of Egyptian Religion*, p. 201. Cf. also K. Sethe, *Untersuchungen z. Geschichte und Altertumskunde Aegyptens*, ii. 3.

known Step-Pyramid of Sakkarah (Fig. III), near
Memphis, and familiar to every tourist who
ascends the Nile.[1]　This pyramid, a transition
between the mastaba tombs of the earlier kings
and the true pyramid form which is met with
later, was constructed by the superimposition of
five successively smaller mastabas on an original
large one.　The east and west sides of the base
measured 396 feet in length, and the north and
south sides 352 feet, while the height was about
195 feet.　The six gigantic steps measure in height
38, 36, 34½, 32, 31, and 29½ feet respectively, while
the width of each step is from 6 to 7 feet.　Within
the building, which was constructed of blocks of
limestone, the halls and corridors were lined with
blue and green glazed tiles of inlaid faience,
bearing the King's names and titles.[2]　This
pyramid is the earliest large stone structure known
to history, and was destined to become the tomb
of King Zoser.[3]

[1] The Arab name ' Sakkarah ' is probably a corruption of
an older Egyptian word Sokari (Socharis), the name of an
early god of the dead at Memphis.

[2] An illustration of one of these halls decorated with tiles
is given by Maspero, *Manua of Egyptian Archaeology*, 1914,
p. 303.

[3] Zoser began by building a mastaba tomb at Bet-Khallâf
near Abydos, and subsequently abandoned this scheme in
favour of the more ambitious pyramid which was constructed
of hewn stone instead of bricks.

III.   THE STEP-PYRAMID OF SAKKARAH

The Step-Pyramid of Sakkarah [1] is further an index of a high state of civilization. There must have been wealth in the Pharaonic exchequer, stable government by the vizier and other officials, experience in the organization of labour, aptitude in the keeping of complex accounts, technical skill in the quarrying, dressing, and transportation of stone. In all these indications of economic prosperity we may see in part at least the genius of the vizier Imhotep. Nor can we doubt that the triumphant completion of the first pyramid, the earliest large monument constructed of hewn stone, must have paved the way for the yet mightier pyramids that were soon to follow.

The name of Imhotep is also associated with the first temple of Edfu which was said to have been constructed according to a plan dropped down from heaven to earth near the city of Memphis. ' The master craftsman was Imhotep, the son of Ptah, the great god of Memphis, and father

[1] The conception of the terraced pyramid of Sakkarah appears on first thoughts a stroke of genius on the part of King Zoser and his architect Imhotep. There are, however, somewhat similar square monuments in India and Mesopotamia of remote antiquity known as Stupas, Topes, or Dagobas, which may have suggested the idea of Sakkarah. There may well have been occasional communications between Egypt and the East even under the early Dynasties. Cf. W. Simpson, ' The Tower of Babel, and the Birs Nimroud, *Transactions of the S. of Biblical Archaeology*, 1893, ix, p. 307.

and son united their powers and produced the first temple at Edfu in one of the earliest periods of Egyptian history.' [1]

The present splendid temple (Fig. IV) was begun during the reign of Ptolemy III Euergetes I, 237 B. C., and finished in 57 B. C. The inscriptions in the temple describe Imhotep ' as the great priest Imhotep the son of Ptah, who speaks or lectures '.[2]

As we shall see in greater detail farther on, Imhotep appears to have been the second member of a long pedigree of architects, commencing with his father Kanofer (cf. Appendix C), and ending with Khnum-ib-re, who was chief minister of works for the whole country, and architect of Upper and Lower Egypt from the twenty-seventh to the thirtieth year of King Darius I (*ca.* 490 B. C.).

C. Imhotep as Chief Lector Priest
or *Kheri-heb*

Imhotep held the important office of *Kheri-heb her tep*, 𓊆𓂋𓏤𓈖𓏛, or first lector priest.[3] In

---

[1] E. A. Budge, *A History of Egypt*, 1902, viii, p. 49.

[2] De Rougé, *Inscriptions et Notices du Temple d'Edfou*, ii, Pl. 89. Cf. also Appendix E. According to Naville, *Textes relatifs au Mythe d'Horus à Edfou*, 1870, p. 15, this is the only monument which contains the signature of the artist who made its plan.

[3] An excellent account of the Egyptian priesthood by A. M.

IV. THE TEMPLE OF EDFU

this capacity his duty was to recite from the holy books, and since according to the Egyptian faith these religious texts possessed magical powers, the common people regarded the *Kheri-heb* as a magician.

The *Kheri-heb* took an important part in ceremonies known as the ' Liturgy of Funerary Offerings ' dealing with the presentation of gifts to the dead, the formula which was pronounced over each element being supposed to change it into a divine and spiritual food, which was partaken of by the souls of the departed. The material elements of the offerings were eaten by the priests and by the relatives of the deceased, who were thus brought into communion with the blessed dead and with the gods.[1] Although the formulas in the liturgy were recited by the *Kheri-heb* priest, who held in his hands a roll of papyrus and directed the assistant priests, most of the ceremonies were performed by the *Sem* priest, ⌐⌐, assisted by several ministrants.

In the other series of ceremonies known as ' The Opening the Mouth ', ⌣, the object was

Blackman will be found in the *Encyclopaedia of Religion and Ethics*, x, p. 294. E. A. Budge (*Gods of the Egyptians*, i, p. 525) states that Imhotep was attached to the priesthood of Re, the sun-god.

[1] E. A. Budge, *The Liturgy of Funerary Offerings*, pp. ix, 41 ff.

to restore to the inert corpse the functions of which it had been deprived by death and embalmment. The mouth was symbolically opened that the mummy might speak, and the eyes touched that they might see. A bull was slaughtered in order to provide food, while other ceremonies were intended to enable clothes, unguents, &c., to be used, in fact to cause the mummy in all respects to resemble a living human body. The end in view was also aimed at by the recitation of appropriate formulas and by touching the mummy case with a wand shaped like the hieroglyph ⌐. When these ceremonies had been performed the body was lowered into the grave and the approach closed, a funeral feast being held in the ante-chamber of the tomb.

Here also the *Kheri-heb* was responsible for the order of ritual,[1] although he had various assistants, especially the *Sem*[2] who in many respects played the principal part. In brief the *Kheri-heb*

[1] E. A. Budge, *The Book of Opening the Mouth*, p. 11 and *passim*. In both these series of ceremonies the details date mainly from the XVIIIth Dynasty ; but most of them were certainly of much earlier origin.

[2] In the ceremony of ' The Opening of the Mouth ' at the tomb of Amenemhēt the principal part is played by the *Sem* priest, the role of the *Kheri-heb* being that of prompter to his companions. Cf. A. H. Gardiner, *The Tomb of Amenemhēt*, 1915, pp. 57 ff.; Maspero, *Études de Mythologie et d'Archéologie*, i, pp. 283–324.

was held in great honour throughout Egypt. By the common people he was regarded as the mediator between the King and the unseen powers of the universe, and was supposed to influence the final destinies of the dead.[1]

There is an interesting reference to Imhotep in the Ritual of Embalmment. After the statement that the deceased sees Ammon, the text goes on to say to him :

' Thy soul unites itself to Imhotep whilst thou art in the funeral valley, and thy heart rejoiceth because thou dost not go into the dwelling of Sebek,[2] and because thou art like a son in the house of his father, and doest what pleaseth thee in the city of Thebes.' [3]

[1] To Imhotep were also attributed in later times the words of power which protected the dead from all kinds of enemies that awaited them in the Underworld or Duat (Ṭuat) ★ 𓅓 𓏭. Without such words of power poor persons who could not purchase even cheap amulets or afford costly funerals might be unable to continue their way through the later stages of the Underworld. E. A. Budge, *Gods of the Egyptians*, i, pp. 261, 523.

[2] The Crocodile god Sebek was associated in certain of his aspects with the idea of death and destruction. This allusion therefore probably means that the deceased would escape annihilation.

[3] Maspero, *Mémoire sur quelques Papyrus du Louvre*, 1875, pp. 24, 80. The papyrus is written in hieratic and is of late (Graeco-Roman) date.

D. IMHOTEP AS SAGE AND SCRIBE

Imhotep enjoyed the reputation of being ' one of the greatest of Egyptian sages ' ;[1] his fame for wisdom made so deep an impression on his countrymen that it endured as a national tradition for many centuries.

As regards his literary activities, he is said to have produced works on medicine and architecture, as well as on more general subjects, and some of his works were extant at the dawn of the Christian era. His proverbs, embodying the philosophy of life which experience had taught, were handed down from generation to generation, and were noted for their grace and poetic diction, their author being described as a ' master of poetry '. We shall see later on that his eminence as a man of letters led him to be recognized as the ' patron of scribes '.

An interesting song, or rather dirge, known as the ' Song of the Harper ',[2] has survived in which

---

[1] E. A. Budge, *Short History of Egypt*, p. 91.

[2] A complete copy of the song occurs in the Harris Papyrus, No. 500 in the British Museum, and a copy was also inscribed on the walls of the Theban Tomb of Pa-aten-em-hab (XVIIIth Dynasty) of which the remaining fragments are now at Leiden. (Leemans, *Monuments*, Pt. III, Pl. xii ; conveniently reproduced in Breasted, *History of Egypt*, 1919, p. 208.) A similar song is inscribed on the walls of the

the names of Imhotep and Hordedef [1] are linked together and in which these two sages dilate on the uncertainty and brevity of life, and enforce the doctrine that as man is so soon gone and forgotten, he should enjoy his life to the full. The philosophy is that of those persons who in all ages of the world have said: 'Let us eat and drink, for to-morrow we die.' [2] This poem was evidently a great favourite. The oldest version that has survived was written in the tomb of the Theban King Antuf [3] near the figure of the harper, and was doubtless sung during the funeral feast for the entertainment of the guests. The object was to remind them of the brevity of life, even while they were enjoying it.[4] The following version

Theban tomb of Neferhotpe. Both have been studied in detail and published by Maspero, *Études Égyptiennes*, i, pp. 172 ff.

[1] Hordedef was a prince of the IVth Dynasty and probably a son of Khufu (Cheops) , the builder of the great pyramid of Gizeh. He also was one of the wise men of Egypt and figures in the famous story of Khufu and the magicians.

[2] 1 Corinthians xv. 32.

[3] King Antuf (Intef) was one of the kings of the XIth Dynasty. There were some other kings Antuf in the XVIIth Dynasty.

[4] Herodotus (ii. 78) thus describes this striking custom among the Egyptians: 'In the social banquets of the rich, as soon as the feast is ended, a man carries round a wooden figure of a corpse in its coffin, graven and painted so as to

conveys a good impression of this poem and indicates the feeling and rhythm met with in Egyptian literature, although there are no rhyming lines :

> *Song of the House of the Blessed King Antuf,
> which is written in front of the Harper.*[1]

ALL hail to the prince, the good man,
Whose body must pass away,
While his children remain for aye.

The gods of old rest in their tombs,
And the mummies of men long dead ;
The same for both rich and poor.

The words of Imhotep I hear,
The words of Hordedef, which say :
' What is prosperity ? tell ! '

Their fences and walls are destroyed,
Their houses exist no more ; [2]
And no man cometh again from the tomb
To tell of what passeth below.

resemble the reality as nearly as possible, from one to two cubits long. And as he shows it to each of the guests, he says, " Look on this, and drink, and be merry ; for when thou art dead, such shalt thou be." '

[1] H. R. Hall, *Cambridge Ancient History*, i, p. 324 ; Erman, *Life in Ancient Egypt*, p. 386 ; W. Max Müller, *Die Liebespoesie der alten Aegypter*, pp. 29, 35.

[2] This allusion to the walls and house of Imhotep is peculiarly effective. Although he was the famous architect of King Zoser, yet his own tomb has so entirely disappeared that ' the place thereof knows it no more '.

Ye go to the place of the mourners,
To the bourne whence none return ;
Strengthen your hearts to forget your joys,
Yet fulfil your desires while ye live.

Anoint yourselves, clothe yourselves well,
Use the gifts which the gods bestow,
Fulfil your desires upon earth.

For the day will come to you all
When ye hear not the voices of friends,
When weeping avails you no more.

So feast in tranquillity now,
For none taketh his goods below to the tomb,
And none cometh thence back again.

It would of course not be fair to judge of
Imhotep's philosophy from so slender a basis as
that presented by the ' Song of the Harper '. As
his reputation was so enduring, there were doubtless precepts and proverbs enjoining a higher
morality. His name is sometimes linked with
those of two other famous Egyptian sages, i. e.
Kegemni who lived in the reign of Huni, last
king of the IIIrd Dynasty, and Ptah-hotpe,
vizier of King Assa, of the Vth Dynasty, both
of whom have bequeathed precepts of singular
beauty.

We append one gem from the ' Instruction of
Ptah-hotpe', which teaches the virtue of humility :

' If thou be great, after being of none account,
and hast gotten riches after squalor, being fore-

most of these in the city, and hast knowledge concerning useful matters, so that promotion is come to thee ; then swathe not thine heart in thine own hoard, for thou art become the steward of the endowments of the god.' [1]

It is delightful to have voices speaking across so long a span of years and recalling the philosophy held by the wise men of an ancient nation, whose glory has now departed.

E.   IMHOTEP AS ASTRONOMER

If the references to Imhotep in Hermetic literature can be trusted, he was also interested in astronomy and astrology, although no special observations are associated with his name. Sethe gives various references to that literature, showing that Imhotep was reputed to have been associated with the god Thoth (Hermes) in astronomical observations.[2] Doubtless he was a believer in the influence exerted by the heavenly bodies on the welfare of men, as was the fashion in the Pharaonic period.

The faith that stars in their courses powerfully affected human destiny was wellnigh universal, and this faith led to a close study of the movements of the heavenly bodies, of eclipses, of the

[1] B. Gunn, *The Instruction of Ptah-Hotep, and the Instruction of Kegemni: the Oldest Books of the World*, p. 54.

[2] Sethe, *Imhotep*, p. 22.

precession of the equinoxes, of occultations of the planets, of the length of the sidereal year, as well as to the identification of the sun, moon and stars with the principal deities in the Egyptian pantheon. Both the sun and moon were the objects of divine worship by the royal family and the nobles, as some of the grandest of natural objects.[1] No wonder that the fundamental laws of astronomy were discovered and brought into intimate association both with national events and with the ordinary occurrences of life.

As Diodorus Siculus says : ' There is no country where the positions and movements of the stars have been observed with such accuracy as in Egypt. Registers in which these observations are recorded have been kept during an incredible number of years.' [2]

F. Imhotep as a Magician-Physician

Imhotep enjoyed a high reputation both as magician and as physician. He was ' a famous priest and magician of Memphis ',[3] while his

---

[1] The common people worshipped their local gods.

[2] Diodorus Siculus, Book I, c. L, LXXXI. Cf. Herodotus, ii. 4. Of the native Egyptian records of the movements of the heavenly bodies, the most celebrated are those in the royal tombs at Thebes. Cf. Le Page Renouf, *Life-Work*, iii, pp. 97 ff.

[3] E. A. Budge, *The Literature of the Ancient Egyptians*, p. 84.

subsequent apotheosis as the god of medicine testifies to his skill as a healer of the sick. We may briefly refer here to the twin offices of magician and physician, leaving a fuller discussion of the subject to an *excursus* on early Egyptian medicine.

Magic and medicine were closely allied in the time of the Pharaohs. Magic is generally regarded as the older of the two and never lost hold on her offspring. By magic actions are implied such actions as persons perform for their own or others' benefit and which demand certain mysterious and miraculous powers for their performance. According to the Egyptian belief, wizardry could work all kinds of wonders which were not possible by simple means.[1]

The operations of magic related to all the events of daily life. It might be prophylactic of evil, curative of disease, prognostic of calamity, sometimes benevolent towards others, at other times malevolent. One common characteristic was the use of a mystic incomprehensible gibberish to convey an impression of wisdom behind it. It is difficult to draw any hard-and-fast line between religion and magic, since the latter was in large measure a form of applied religion (*religio privata*). Practitioners of magic kept a box of materials and instruments always ready so as to

[1] Cf. the article on ' Magic ' by A. H. Gardiner, *Encyclopaedia of Religion and Ethics*, viii, p. 262.

apply their art to any special circumstances that arose.[1]

In the Westcar Papyrus [2] allusion is made to a wonderful feat of magic performed by the chief *Kheri-heb* or lector priest of King Zoser, who, it has been suggested, may well have been Imhotep.[3] The full details are not told, but the allusion occurs in a speech made to the King Khufu (Cheops) by one of his sons as having occurred in the days of King Zoser and performed by his chief lector priest.

Although Imhotep was a noted magician, it appears that medicine was the mistress he most zealously wooed ; it is his eminence as a healer of the sick that has given him imperishable fame, and that led eventually to his deification. For a time he was court physician to King Zoser, whose vizier he had been ; evidently he moved in the highest social circles.

Doubtless magic and medicine were closely associated in his treatment of the sick, the remedy most suited to the malady in question being

[1] Magic was practised in England not so many years ago and even to-day is not extinct. Cf. Elworthy, *The Evil Eye*, 1895, pp. 53, 56 ; C. K. Sharpe, *Witchcraft in Scotland*, 1884, p. 21.

[2] Erman, *Die Märchen des Papyrus Westcar*, i, p. 7. The Westcar Papyrus contains in the form of a popular romance an account of the wonders wrought by magicians for the entertainment of King Khufu (Cheops).

[3] Sethe, *Imhotep*, p. 25.

selected. Magical papyri are leavened with medical prescriptions, while medical papyri, such as the Ebers Papyrus, are constantly interspersed with incantations.

Unhappily, nothing is known of his special work as a physician. The important office of vizier must have added prestige to his name and inspired confidence in his patients. But the fact that he later on received divine honours—a rare event except in the case of a king—proves him to have been a man of rare distinction. A fine type of scholar-physician, he evidently rendered service both to the bodies and spirits of the sick and afflicted to whom it was his privilege to minister.

As regards Imhotep's relations, a few details have come down to us (cf. Appendix C). His father was a famous court architect or master-builder named Kanofer 𓏛𓏛𓏛 *Kꜣ-nfr*. This we learn from an inscription found in the Wadi Hammamat, a valley leading from Coptos down to the Red Sea, and giving a genealogical tree of the ancestors of the architect Chnem-eb-re (Khnum-ib-re).

Much less is known about Imhotep's mother Khreduonkh 𓏛𓏛𓏛 *Ḥrdw-ꜥnḫ* and his wife Ronpe-nofret 𓏛𓏛𓏛 *Rnpt-nfrt*. After his apotheosis, his mother Khreduonkh was looked upon as the mother of a god, and was represented with a human head, adorned with the hood of a vulture and with double feathers.[1] His wife Ronpe-nofret likewise after the apotheosis of her husband became the wife of a god.

The Egyptians appear to have found no difficulty in regarding Imhotep as the son of the god Ptah, while his mother, wife and other relations were but ordinary mortals.[2] Such double filiation was possible since deities could borrow a human body so as to enable a woman to bear them a son. Imhotep could thus be the son both of Ptah and of Kanofer.

We have no information as to the length of

[1] Sethe, *Imhotep*, pp. 4, 24.

[2] The names Imhotep, Kanofer, and Ronpe-nofret were not uncommon under the Old Kingdom, while that of Khreduonkh does not appear till the Graeco-Roman period. One of the Pharaohs was named Imhotep, although the date of his reign is uncertain. At Berlin is preserved the stela of a man named Imhotep, who in one picture is seen praying before Osiris, in another before Osiris-Apis. A. Erman, *Handbook of Egyptian Religion*, p. 217.

The mastaba-tomb of another man named Imhotep, a famous official of one of the XIIth Dynasty kings named Sesostris (Senusert), was discovered at the South Pyramid of Lisht in 1914. *Ancient Egypt*, 1915, p. 146.

Another Imhotep, who bore the titles ' Royal Scribe ' and ' Child of the Nursery ', lived at Thebes in the reign of Amenophis III (*ca.* 1410–1375 B. C.). Persons of the same name are also mentioned by Brugsch, *Z. f. Ägyptische Sprache*, 1884, xxii, pp. 118 ff.

In ancient Egypt there appears to have been a fortress called the ' Gate of Imhotep '. Erman and Ranke, *Aegypten*,

E

Imhotep's life or the date of his death. As far as history goes he was a man of high and un-sullied character, with a wide outlook on life, as well as a tender heart towards suffering humanity. We may therefore well be confident that when, after a career devoted to the public service, to the healing of the sick, and to his many other interests, he was at length laid to rest, a great concourse of mourners joined in the funeral procession and accompanied the mummy to its last home. Moreover, with the knowledge we possess of the funerary ceremonial in the early dynasties, and with a little imagination, we can readily picture to ourselves the various episodes on the way to the vast necropolis of Memphis.

After the embalmment of the body, a process which occupied several weeks, the corpse would be placed in a four-sided somewhat plain coffin which was then covered with flowers and ferried across the Nile on a richly decorated barque, accompanied by several other boats filled with friends and relations. Meanwhile the funerary priest, i.e. the *Kheri-heb*, made offerings and burnt incense before the mummy, and conducted his official recitations and invocations to the gods.[1]

1923, p. 628. Roeder suggests that this may perhaps have been built by the subject of this monograph (Pauly, *Real-Encyclopädie*, ix. 1213).

[1] Many details and illustrations of funeral ceremonies will

The river safely crossed, the coffin together with its barque was transferred to a sledge and drawn by oxen to the already constructed mastaba, every stage of the journey being accompanied by a complicated ceremonial. Egyptian mourners were highly demonstrative and in the case of Imhotep doubtless there was pathetic wailing of his friends and relations, as well as of the sick and afflicted patients to whom he had formerly ministered. Especially affected would be the women who with bare breasts uttered impassioned cries, slapped their faces, and scattered ashes on their heads, everything being done to glorify the deceased and to indicate the grievous loss and solitude of the survivors.

Imhotep's mastaba, which will doubtless some day be unearthed, was probably situated in the desert just outside the city of Memphis, near to the Serapeum and the modern village of Abusir. It was therefore also close to the famous pyramid which the deceased had built for his patron and royal master Zoser.[1] Near to this spot was later on situated the Pi-î-m-hotp-si-ptah

be found in Erman and Ranke, *Aegypten*, 1923, pp. 344 ff. Cf. also Maspero, *Études Égyptiennes*, 1886, i, pp. 81–194.

[1] Since these pages have been in the press, excavations carried on at Sakkarah by Mr. C. M. Firth, of the ' Service des Antiquités ', have brought to light some remarkable buildings constructed by Imhotep. They consist of a wall

' the temple of Imhotep, son of Ptah ',[1] which the Greeks called ' the Asklepieion '.[2]

As we shall see in the next Chapters it was not Imhotep's destiny to lie forgotten in one of the numerous mastabas in the necropolis of Memphis, in which repose so many notable Egyptians. A far higher distinction awaited him than any Pharaoh could confer, for posterity raised him to the rank of the Egyptian deity of medicine, and gave him a place among the immortals whose name will be held in everlasting honour. *Non moritur cujus fama vivit.*

500 yards long by 300 yards wide, enclosing the Step-Pyramid, together with a beautiful colonnade about 85 yards long, which appears to have formed the main entrance to the pyramid enclosure. There are 48 columns of white limestone arranged in pairs, the shafts being carved so as to imitate a bundle of reeds. Further details, as well as an illustration of the colonnade, will be found in *The Times* of January 16th, 1926.

[1] Brugsch, *Dictionnaire Géographique*, p. 1098.

[2] An ancient writer, Mercur, states that Asklepios, *sc.* Imhotep, was buried at a town called Crocodilopolis, which was probably close to Gebelên, a few miles north of Esnah. By far the strongest evidence, however, points to Sakkarah as the place of sepulture, where the Step-Pyramid of King Zoser is situated. Weigall, on the other hand, does not wholly discredit the Gebelên suggestion. ' If the hills of Gebelên ', he writes, ' contain Imhotep's tomb, their interest to the visitor will not be lessened by the fact that they hold the bones of the earliest philosopher and wise man known to the world's history.' A. E. Weigall, *Guide to the Antiquities of Upper Egypt*, 1913, p. 298.

III

IMHOTEP AS MEDICAL DEMIGOD

FOR many years Egyptologists have been puzzled to explain why Imhotep, who lived in the days of King Zoser, *ca.* 2900 B.C., was not ranked among the full gods of Egypt until the Persian period, dating from 525 B.C. The apotheosis of a man, however distinguished, so many centuries after his life on earth seems indeed mysterious. The explanation appears to be that first suggested by Erman, viz. that Imhotep, at any rate during a large part of the interval, was regarded as a sort of hero or demigod and received a semi-divine worship. Erman suggested that this rank of demigod was bestowed on him at the time of the New Kingdom, i.e. about 1580 B.C., but more recent evidence seems to indicate that this demigod stage was reached at a much earlier period.

In one of the Oxyrhynchus Papyri, written in Greek, and dating probably from the second century A.D.,[1] we read that King Mycerinus ⟨◎⚏⚏⟩, the son of Khufu (Cheops) of the

---

[1] Grenfell and Hunt, *Oxyrhynchus Papyri*, Part XI (1915). Cf. also *Ancient Egypt*, 1916, p. 41. This Papyrus, itself a copy, was found in the temple of Imhotep in the time of Nectanebo. It possesses great interest, although opinions

IVth Dynasty, established temples and endowments for Imhotep the son of Ptah and other persons.[1] Consequently, if this Papyrus is to be trusted, Imhotep was worshipped as early as the IVth Dynasty, and his temple was resorted to by sick and afflicted persons.

The writer of the Papyrus, named Nechautis, worked up the story of Imhotep from the record found in his temple, with the object of showing that he, the writer, was the proper person to hold the office of priest of Imhotep with power to bequeath that position to his posterity.[2] He further states that he had resolved to honour Imhotep by translating into Greek an ancient Egyptian work he had before him, but that he feared to undertake the task lest he might prove unable to do justice to the merits of the deity. He hoped that, when older and more experienced, he might be better equipped for the work. Then

may differ as to its reliability as an historical document ; attributions of great antiquity to religious foundations must be accepted with reserve. On the other hand, Grenfell and Hunt write : ' So far as it goes, the evidence of this Papyrus favours the view that the worship of Imhotep began in the early days of Egyptian History.'

[1] The other persons are Horus son of Hermes, and Kaleoibis son of Apollo ; it is not known who these were.

[2] Some offices in the priesthood were hereditary and attached to certain families. Cf. Erman and Ranke, *Aegypten*, 1923, p. 331.

V. IMHOTEP AS A DEMIGOD

follows the story of a vision in which Imhotep (Asklepios) appears to a devotee, which throws such a vivid light on the Egyptian temple as a resort of the sick and on the practice of incubation that it is worth reproducing at some length.[1]

The story relates to the mother of Nechautis who was attacked with quartan ague, which induced her friends to seek assistance at the temple of Imhotep. This deity appeared to the sick woman in dreams and cured her by ' simple remedies ', for which both mother and son showed their thanks by sacrifices.

Nechautis himself subsequently also fell ill, with pain in his right side, violent fever, loss of breath and coughing, associated with the pain in his side. He too, in his turn, and accompanied by his mother, hastened to the shrine and lapsed into half-unconscious sleep. Meanwhile his mother, wide awake, suddenly perceived in a vision a being of superhuman stature,[2] clothed in shining raiment and carrying a book, who regarded the patient intently from head to foot and then vanished. When the mother had re-

[1] For fuller details reference must be made to Grenfell and Hunt's translation. An excellent *résumé* of the story appears in the *Lancet*, 1915, ii, p. 1204.

[2] When a deity appeared to a mortal his divinity was shown by his superhuman stature.

covered from her surprise at the vision, she woke
up the invalid and found that his fever had
departed, leaving him in a profuse perspiration.
As soon as the invalid was able to speak he began
to recount what he had seen in a dream, i.e. the
same vision that his mother had witnessed whilst
awake. The pains in his side soon ceased, the
god having given him an ' assuaging cure '.

The mother and son at once proceeded to
express their gratitude by the customary sacrifices
and, it may be presumed, ' donaria '. Imhotep,
however, notified that such were not the recom-
pense and signs of gratitude he required. He
wished Nechautis to fulfil the promise made
years ago to re-edit the ancient Egyptian book
in Greek.

The writer then goes on to say that, since the
divine master regretted the non-composition of
the divine book, which invoked his providence
and was filled with the story of his divinity and
inventiveness, he set about the dutiful task, which
he thus describes :

' Since thou hadst once noticed, Master, that
I was neglecting the divine book invoking thy
providence and filled with thy divinity, I hastened
to the inspired task of the history. And I hope
to extend by my proclamation the fame of thy
inventiveness ; for I unfolded truly by a physical
treatise in another book the convincing account

VI. IMHOTEP AS A DEMIGOD

of the creation of the world. Throughout I have
filled up defects and struck out superfluities. . . .
Hence, Master, I conjecture the book has been
completed in accordance with thy favour, . . .
suiting thy divinity. As the discoverer of this
art, Asclepios,[1] greatest of Gods and my teacher,
thou art distinguished by the thanks of all men.
For every gift of a votive offering or sacrifice
presently perishes, but a written record is an
undying meed of gratitude, renewing its youth
in the memory. Every Greek tongue will tell
thy story and every man will worship the son of
Ptah, Imouthes.'

The address closes with the following proclamation :

' Assemble all ye benevolent and good persons !
Depart all wicked and godless ones ! Assemble
all ye . . . who have been cured of diseases through
serving the god, all ye who practise the healing art,
all ye who zealously strive after a virtuous life, ye
who in the past have been blessed with abundance
of good things, ye who have been delivered from
the perils of the sea ! For every place has been
penetrated by the saving grace of the god.'

The text then proceeds to recount the history

[1] i. e. Imhotep. This is an illustration of the concealment
of an Egyptian deity under a Greek name. The quotation
also throws an interesting light on the system of propaganda
practised by the devotees of Imhotep. Every effort was
made, both by word of mouth and by written records, to
broadcast any marvellous cures, in order further to enhance
the prestige of the god of healing. Cf. W. Schubart, *Ägypten
von Alexander dem Grossen bis auf Mohammed*, p. 314.

of Asklepios (Imhotep), son of Hephaestos,[1] and
the manner in which he told Mycerinus to busy
himself with his tomb. It is clear that though
Imhotep was not yet recognized as a full deity,
he was to some extent worshipped in the same
manner as a god.[2]

Until the Oxyrhynchus Papyrus described
above was discovered showing that Imhotep was
worshipped in the time of King Mycerinus his
elevation to the status of demigod had been
associated with the religious revival that occurred
at the advent of the New Kingdom, i.e. 1580
B. C.[3] One result of this revival was a resuscitation
of ancient beliefs and cults accompanied by a more
elaborate and magnificent ritual at the services.
The gods came to be enthroned in palatial
temples that glistened with costly sacramental
vessels, the ceremonies being supported by
wealthy endowments, while the high priests
enjoyed wellnigh royal rank and power.

This increase in the magnificence and wealth
of the great Egyptian gods led more and more
to their estrangement from the common people.

[1] The fact that Hephaestos is here equated with Ptah
indicates the late date of the Papyrus. Milne states that there
is a mixed Graeco-Egyptian coin-type of Ptah-Hephaistos
(*History of Egypt under Roman Rule*, 1924, p. 193).

[2] K. Sethe, *Encyclopaedia of Religion and Ethics*, vi, p. 647.

[3] Cf. Erman, *A Handbook of Egyptian Religion*, 1907, p. 56,
Ch. on ' Religious Beliefs and Customs of the New Kingdom '.

VII. IMHOTEP AS A DEMIGOD

The humble peasant felt that he could no longer approach his deity with his daily petitions for body and soul, as he used to do in more primitive times. Yet the common people seem as much as before to have needed a superhuman helper and friend in sympathy with the troubles and problems of life and accessible to their personal needs. Thus came about the introduction of new and more popular deities, or rather of demigods, heroes, or saints, who could be worshipped and invoked by the common people, and these were often selected from amongst the national heroes of past ages. Among them was the wise and good Imhotep.[1]

These popular demigods were probably regarded somewhat as the Greeks later on revered their hero-gods to whom was rendered a semi-divine worship.[2]

[1] These popular deities (*Sondergötter*—German) later on obtained important places in the Pantheon. Cf. A. Wiedemann, *Encyclopaedia of Religion and Ethics*, vi, p. 276.

A parallel may be cited in the case of the Pharaoh Amenophis I (XVIIIth Dynasty), who was deified after his death and considerably later became the local patron of that quarter of Thebes in which the necropolis workmen lived. These men resorted to this deified king for help and advice in all their troubles.

[2] An excellent summary of the question is given by K. Sethe (*Imhotep*, p. 4, and in the *Encyclopaedia of Religion and Ethics*, vi, p. 650). It is interesting to note that both in Greece and in Rome a ' demigod ' stage was recognized on the way to full apotheosis. Julius Caesar became a demigod before being

Erman writes :

' Out of this esteem for the ancient wisdom there arose the veneration manifested at this late time for those who had been leaders of the nation in the primitive period. They had previously been looked upon as people of renown, now some of them were regarded as demigods. . . . Among them is Imhotep, a man who belonged to the court of Zoser, one of the earliest of the Kings of Egypt, and who was remembered by the people as the celebrated royal architect, and as the author of ancient literature.' [1]

This view of the demigod stage being deferred till the New Kingdom depends, however, on the opinion that is formed of the trustworthiness of the Oxyrhynchus Papyrus referred to above.

It is also during this demigod stage, in the XVIIIth Dynasty (Amenophis III), that arose the custom amongst Egyptian scribes of pouring a libation out of their water-bowl to ' that most famous of scribes ' Imhotep.[2] A. H. Gardiner thus refers to this custom :

' That Imhotep should have been so distinguished from other Egyptian celebrities by a

enrolled amongst the gods. Smith, *Dictionary of Greek and Roman Antiquities*, 1901, i, pp. 140–1.

[1] A. Erman, *Handbook of Egyptian Religion*, 1907, p. 173. Cf. also Erman and Ranke, *Aegypten*, 1923, p. 378, where Erman speaks of ' the demigod Imhotep, the son of the goddess Sechmet '.

[2] *Z. f. Ägyptische Sprache*, xxxvi, 1898, p. 147 ; xl, 1902–3, p. 146.

special rite, not the common funeral offering accorded to others, is surely sufficient to warrant the epithet demigod, not denied him at a later date.'

In the numerous bronze statuettes (Figs. I, v–vii) representing the demigod stage of his career [1] Imhotep presents obvious signs of his human origin (Appendix D). He appears in the figure of an ordinary man, clothed in the simple garments of primitive days, without sceptre or ankh or the peculiar beard worn by the gods.[2] He looks like a sage and is generally seated on a throne or chair, rarely standing, and with a roll of papyrus on his knees or under his arm ; he may either be reading or appear to be buried in thought.

This appearance forms a striking contrast to that met with after his apotheosis, as we shall see in the next Chapter.

[1] Figs. I, v, vi, vii represent Imhotep as a demigod. Nos. I and v are taken from the *Catalogue des Antiquités Égyptiennes du Musée du Caire : Statues de Divinités*, i, p. 17 ; ii, Pl. iv. No. vi is a statuette preserved in the Wellcome Historical Medical Museum, London, and is remarkable for the row of uraei arranged round the seat as a decoration. No. vii is in the Berlin Staats-Museum.

[2] Erman, *Handbook of Egyptian Religion*, 1907, p. 174.

IV

THE APOTHEOSIS OF IMHOTEP AS
GOD OF MEDICINE

THE full apotheosis of Imhotep (Figs. VIII, IX, and X) appears to have taken place in the Persian period,[1] somewhere about 525 B.C., the year in which Egypt was conquered by Cambyses and became a Persian province.[2] To this new

[1] The three Figs. VIII, IX, and X represent Imhotep as the full deity of medicine. No. VIII shows the god in the standing posture and carrying the uas sceptre in one hand and the ankh in the other ; it is taken from the temple of Ptah at Karnak (p. 57). No. IX shows him in a sitting posture and is taken from the temple of Medinet Habu (p. 57). No. X is a mutilated bronze statuette preserved at the British Museum. It shows the figure of Imhotep carrying an ankh in his left hand, while the broken-off right arm is extended and appears as if it originally held a sceptre. This appears to be the only known statuette showing Imhotep as a full deity. Its date has been conjectured to be the XXVIth Dynasty. But the variations in the figure from the conventional XXVIth to the Ptolemaic Dynasties, such as the style of the skirt and the coarseness of the legs, point almost certainly to the Roman period.

[2] According to Sethe (*Imhotep*, p. 1), the earliest monument that refers to Imhotep as a deity and that can be approximately dated appears to be the statue of one of his priests named Amasis which is now in the Berlin Museum (No. 14765), and which belongs to the Persian period, *ca.* 525 B.C. According

Egyptian god is now assigned a divine father
Ptah, in place of his human father Kanofer, and
he becomes a member of the great triad of Memphis (Fig. xi), which includes Ptah, Sekhmet, and
Imhotep.[1] His mother Khreduonkh and his

to the inscription on this monument, the great-grandfather
of the priest Amasis who was called Neferebre had filled the
office of third prophet of the house of Imhotep, the son of
Ptah. As this Neferebre is mentioned in conjunction with
the titles King Psammetich II, 594–589 B.C., and must
therefore have been born at latest during his reign, Sethe
concludes that the worship of Imhotep as a deity dates from
the reign of King Amasis (570–525 B.C.). The elevation of
Imhotep to divine rank was probably a gradual process and
unaccompanied by any ceremonial. For the elaborate rites
performed at the deification of Alexander the Great, cf. the
article ' Comment Alexandre devint dieu en Égypte', by
Maspero, *Études de Mythologie et d'Archéologie Égyptiennes*,
1912, vi, p. 263.

[1] Fig. xi. The three figures here shown form the triad of
Memphis : Ptah, Sekhmet, and Imhotep, and are reproduced
from statuettes at the British Museum.

At an earlier period this triad comprised Ptah, Sekhmet,
and Nefertem, but Imhotep appears eventually to have
usurped the place of the latter. The members of Egyptian
triads varied at different times and places. Thus Ptah, Nut,
and Imhotep sometimes form a triad, while in Thebes Ptah,
Mut-Hathor, and Imhotep formed a similar body. Cf. Roscher,
Lexicon, ii (i), p. 125.

According to Brugsch, Imhotep through his association
with Ptah, who in the view of some authorities is one of the
forms of Show (Shu), becomes linked up with the great
Ennead. Cf. Brugsch, *Religion und Mythologie der alten
Aegypter*, pp. 508, 526.

VIII.   IMHOTEP AS DEITY OF MEDICINE

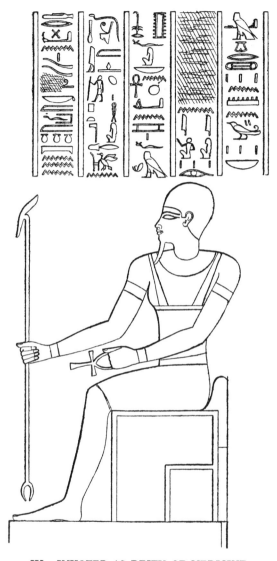

IX. IMHOTEP AS DEITY OF MEDICINE

G

wife Ronpe-nofret are in their turn raised to the
rank of the mother and the wife of a god. The
Graeco-Egyptians called Imhotep Imouthes or
Asklepios and gradually assimilated him with
their own deity of medicine.[1]

The Imhotepian cult was probably at first
associated with his tomb, which, as already
mentioned, was situated outside the city of Memphis on the edge of the desert to the west of
Memphis. As time went on his cult spread far
and wide through the land of Egypt and even
into Nubia. More and more generally was
Imhotep accepted as the deity of medicine, and
worshipped throughout the land, as on a level
with the full gods of Egypt.

A similar process of gradual elevation to the rank
of demigod and finally of full deity occurred in the
case of another noted sage, viz. Amenophis, the
son of Hapi, and vizier to King Amenophis III.
The names of these two sages had lingered for
many centuries in the popular imagination as
national heroes who had in course of time come
to be regarded as superhuman in nature and

[1] This is one of the numerous cases in which under the
influence of Hellenism a fusion took place between Greek and
Egyptian deities. It has even been suggested that the deifi-
cation of Imhotep was due to Hellenistic influence. Cf.
J. G. Milne, *Encyclopaedia of Religion and Ethics*, vi, p. 380 ;
Bissing, *Deutsche Literaturzeitung*, 1902, col. 2330.

X. IMHOTEP AS DEITY OF MEDICINE

therefore entitled to divine honours. Probably in both cases their burial places became centres of pilgrimage, and, at any rate in the case of Imhotep, especially for the sick and suffering. This Amenophis was in many respects the counterpart of Imhotep. What the latter was at the outset for Memphis, Amenophis was for the Thebans down to the latest times. His deification probably took place in the reign of King Ptolemy Euergetes II.[1]

At least three temples are known to have been built in honour of Imhotep. The first one was at Memphis and became a famous hospital and school of magic and medicine.[2] Doubtless countless numbers of sick, maimed, and blind persons resorted to that shrine, and returned to their simple mud hovels nestling under the date palms or amongst the millet fields, full of gratitude for renewed health and strength. This beloved priest-physician was eventually laid to rest near to the temple where he had spent his days in relieving pain and prolonging life. For him we cannot doubt that *sedare dolorem divinum opus*.

[1] H. Brugsch-Bey, *History of Egypt under the Pharaohs*, 1881, i, p. 485 ; K. Sethe, *Encyclopaedia of Religion and Ethics*, vi, p. 651.

[2] Other medical schools existed at Thebes, Sais, and On (Heliopolis). The head priest of Sais bore the title ' Greatest of the Physicians '.

This temple was called by the Greeks the Asklepieion, τὸ πρὸς Μέμφιν μέγα Ἀσκληπιεῖον, and was situated close to the Serapieion. In fact the worship of Imhotep was to some extent connected with that of Serapis, so much so that there were stone altars sacred to him in the Serapieion itself, on which daily libations were offered.[1]

Another temple of Imhotep existed at Philae (Fig. XII) ; of this, a glorious specimen of Egyptian architecture, a large portion has survived to this day, in spite of its immersion in a vast reservoir.[2] Some of the halls (Figs. XIII–XVI) which were used for clinical purposes thousands of years ago are extant.[3]

[1] S. Birch, *Archaeologia*, 1863, xxxix, p. 315.

[2] Fig. XII shows a Plan of the Island of Philae and the position of Imhotep's temple on the island. The temple lies to the south of the much larger temple of Isis which was the principal sanctuary on the island and dedicated to Isis and her son Harpocrates.

[3] Figs. XIII–XVI show the plan and three views of Imhotep's temple. In No. XIII is seen the ground-plan ; in No. XIV the front of the temple ; in No. XV the Western wall and the entrance to the courtyard ; in No. XVI the Eastern wall of the courtyard. It is pleasant to think that Imhotep was worshipped in this famous island, sometimes called the ' Holy Island ', so rich in its associations with religion, with history, with architecture and painting. Kings, conquerors, priests, and travellers without number have been enchanted with its beauty, and have left records of their victories, of their acts of adoration, of their offerings to the deities whose temples still adorn this hallowed spot.

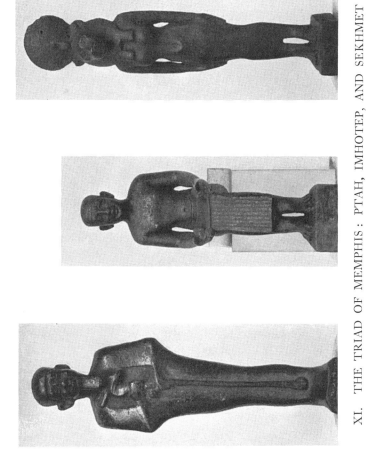

XI. THE TRIAD OF MEMPHIS : PTAH, IMHOTEP, AND SEKHMET

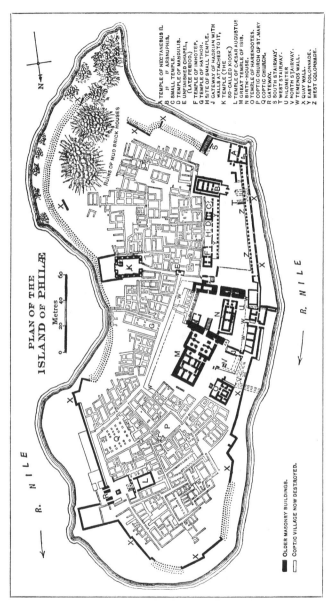

PLAN OF THE
ISLAND OF PHILAE

Metres
0   20   40   60

RUINS OF MUD BRICK HOUSES

R. NILE

R. NILE

A TEMPLE OF NECTANEBUS II.
B   "   "   ARSNUPHIS.
C SMALL TEMPLE.
D TEMPLE OF MANDULIS.
E UNFINISHED CHAPEL,
    (LATE PERIOD.)
F TEMPLE OF IMHOTEP.
G TEMPLE OF HATHOR.
H SITE OF SMALL TEMPLE.
J GATEWAY OF HADRIAN WITH
    WALLS ATTACHED TO IT.
K TEMPLE (THE
    SO-CALLED KIOSK)
L TEMPLE OF CÆSAR AUGUSTUS.
M GREAT TEMPLE OF ISIS.
N BIRTH-HOUSE.
O TEMPLE OF HARENDOTES.
P TEMPLE OF HAREND OF ST.MARY
Q COPTIC CHURCH.
R GATEWAY.
S SOUTH STAIRWAY.
T WEST STAIRWAY.
U NILOMETER.
V NORTH STAIRWAY.
W TEMENOS WALL.
X QUAY WALL.
Y EAST COLONNADE.
Z WEST COLONNADE.

■ OLDER MASONRY BUILDINGS.
☐ COPTIC VILLAGE NOW DESTROYED.

XII.   THE ISLAND OF PHILAE

This temple was built under the Ptolemies, the hieroglyphic inscriptions being those of Ptolemy IV Philopator, while the Greek text over the door, dedicating the building to the Greek god Asklepios, was placed there by the command of Ptolemy V Epiphanes.[1] From one of the former we obtain the following address to Imhotep :

' Great One, Son of Ptah, the creative god, made by Thenen, begotten by him and beloved by him, the god of divine forms in the temples, who giveth life to all men, the mighty one of wonders, the maker of times (?), who cometh unto him that calleth upon him, wheresoever he may be, who giveth sons to the childless, the chief Kheri-heb, the image and likeness of Thoth the Wise.' [2]

The best guide to the temple of Imhotep is the long East Colonnade leading from the temple of

[1] An admirable view of this temple from the south, showing several figures of the deity Imhotep, is given by H. G. Lyons in his *Report on the Island and Temples of Philae*, Pl. x. Cf. also Mahaffy, *History of Egypt under the Ptolemaic Dynasty*, p. 184. As a rule when the Ptolemies erected a temple in honour of their Egyptian gods, its style and ornamentation were purely Egyptian. The Greek inscription at Philae supplies an interesting example of the identification of Imhotep with Asklepios. Budge, *History of Egypt*, viii, p. 133.

[2] Brugsch, *Thesaurus*, p. 783 ; *Religion und Mythologie der alten Aegypter*, p. 527. After his deification Imhotep is sometimes designated as Ibis, i. e. the sacred bird of Thoth. Sages who were raised to the status of divinity were in some measure regarded as incarnations of that god. K. Sethe, *Encyclopaedia of Religion and Ethics*, vi, pp. 650–1.

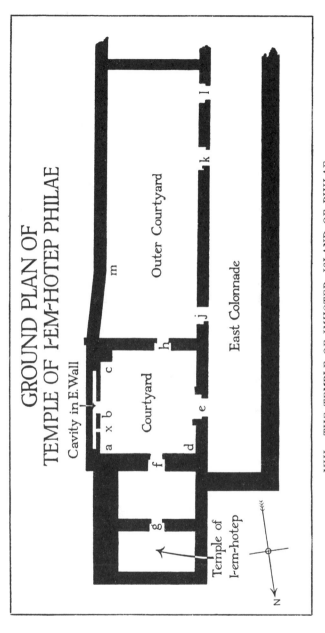

XIII. THE TEMPLE OF IMHOTEP, ISLAND OF PHILAE

GROUND PLAN

Arsnuphis to the Great Pylon, a colonnade con-
sisting of seventeen columns. Through this wall
are cut seven doorways, the first five of which
lead out to the court in which stands the ruined
chapel of Mandulis. The sixth leads to the small
temple of Imhotep.[1] As the visitor passes through
this doorway he finds himself in a little court, on
the north side of which is the entrance to the
temple. There are figures of Imhotep and other
deities on both sides of the entrance which
Weigall thus describes :

' On the left side is seen King Ptolemy V
Epiphanes before Imhotep. On the right side
he is shown before Khnum, Satis and Anukis,
and before Unnefer, Isis and Imhotep. Around
the doorway are small panels of reliefs showing
Osiris, Isis, Khnum, Hathor, Ptah, Thoth and
Imhotep being adored by the King. On either
side of the jambs of the door the King's titles are
inscribed, and reference is made to Isis, while he
is said to be beloved of Imhotep and Ptah.'[2]

There was also a small temple at Thebes, but
it appears to have been less important than that
at Philae. In Thebes, as already mentioned, Ptah,
Mut-Hathor and Imhotep in later times formed

[1] A good plan of these buildings will be found in Baedeker's
Egypt, 1914, p. 365.

[2] A. E. Weigall, *Antiquities of Lower Nubia*, 1907, p. 42.
There are also references to Imhotep and the deities coupled
with him on pp. 40, 43, and 50. Cf. also Weigall's *Antiquities
of Upper Egypt*, 1913, p. 475.

XIV. THE TEMPLE OF IMHOTEP, ISLAND OF PHILAE

FRONT VIEW

XV.   THE TEMPI

The Entrance to the Temple of Imhotep is seen on
The western wall of the Temple (with

TEP, ISLAND OF PHILAE

the first and second columns of the Eastern Colonnade
)orway) occupies the centre of the picture

a triad, which thus differs from the Memphitic triad referred to above, in which Sekhmet formed the third member.[1]

Apart from the temples of Imhotep we have records of a sanatorium which was situated in the upper terrace of the temple of Hatshepsowet at Deir-el-Bahari, and which was given up to the worship of Imhotep and of the other deified hero Amenophis the son of Hapi, both of whom figured at this period as patrons of healing. Under their auspices Deir-el-Bahari seems to have become a regular resort for invalids who scratched or painted numerous invocations to these deities on the walls of the temple.[2]

Amongst common *graffiti* are the following : ' the homage of M. to the lord god Asklepios ' ; ' N. came to worship the great god Asklepios '— usually with the addition of the name Amenothes, and often with that of Hygieia, to Asklepios ; sometimes the writer associated his wife, his family, or his friends in his act of worship.

[1] Brugsch, *Religion und Mythologie der alten Aegypter*, pp. 526–8 ; W. H. Roscher, *Lexicon der Griechischen und Römischen Mythologie*, ii, p. 123. In the period of its glory (XVIIIth–XXth Dynasties) the triad of Thebes consisted of Amon, Mut, and Khons.

[2] J. G. Milne, *J. of Egyptian Archaeology*, 1914, i, p. 96. Cf. also C. R. Piers, *J. of Hellenic Studies*, 1899, xix, p. 13 ; J. G. Milne, *Encyclopaedia of Religion and Ethics*, vi, p. 382. Amenothes is a Greek variant of the more frequent Amenophis.

A *graffito* quoted by Milne is of special interest, as it has been twice improved upon by later commentators. The first entry ran ' Eugraphios offers his homage before the lord god Asklepios and Amenothes and Hygieia : be mindful of us and grant us healing ' ; at the end of this, one Pesubis, presumably a Gnostic who desired some credit to be ascribed to the weird spirits whom he worshipped, wrote ' with the help of Cherstapane and Phritob ' ; finally a Christian, grieved to find so many deities evoked, added his correction above the errors of previous centuries : ' It is the One God who helps you.'

An interesting story has survived which illustrates the practice of incubation at Imhotep's temples. We shall follow here the popular version as emended by Maspero,[1] while readers wishing for a more exact translation are referred to F. Ll. Griffith's transliteration.[2]

The story relates to a man named Satmi Khamuas, the son of the Pharaoh Usermares, who had no man-child by his wife Mahîtuaskhît ; this afflicted him greatly in his heart, and his wife

[1] G. Maspero, *Popular Stories of Ancient Egypt*, 1915, p. 144.

[2] F. Ll. Griffith, *Stories of the High Priests of Memphis*, 1900, pp. 42, 143. Griffith prefers ' Setme ' to ' Satmi ', ' Meh-wesekht ' to ' Mahîtuaskît ', and ' Si-osiri ' to ' Senosiris '.

XVI. THE TEMPLE OF IMHOTEP, ISLAND OF PHILAE

EASTERN WALL OF COURTYARD

Mahîtuaskhît was greatly afflicted with him. One day, when he was more depressed than usual, his wife Mahîtuaskhît went to the temple of Imûthes, son of Ptah, and prayed before him, saying : 'Turn thy face towards me, my lord Imûthes, son of Ptah ; it is thou who dost work miracles, and who art beneficent in all thy deeds ; it is thou who givest a son to her who has none. Listen to my lamentation and give me conception of a man-child.'

Mahîtuaskhît, the wife of Satmi, slept in the temple and she dreamed a dream that same night. One spake with her, saying : 'Art thou not Mahîtuaskhît, the wife of Satmi, who dost sleep in the temple to receive a remedy for thy sterility from the hands of the god ? When to-morrow morning comes, go to the bath-room of Satmi thy husband, and thou wilt find a root of colocasia that is growing there. The colocasia that thou meetest with thou shalt gather with its leaves ; thou shalt make of it a remedy that thou shalt give to thy husband, then thou shalt lie by his side, and thou shalt conceive by him the same night.'

When Mahîtuaskhît awoke from her dream after having seen these things she did everything according to that which had been told her in her dream ; then she lay by the side of Satmi, her

husband, and she conceived by him. When the
time came she had the signs of pregnant women,
and Satmi announced it to Pharaoh, for his heart
rejoiced greatly thereat ; he bound an amulet
upon her (Fig. xvii),[1] and recited a spell over her.
Eventually she gave birth to a remarkable boy
named Senosiris, who later on performed many
wonders in the land of Egypt.

A similar story of sterility being cured by
Imhotep is told in a famous stele of the Ptolemaic
Period, now in the British Museum.[2] The story
relates to a lady named ' Thet Imhotep ', who
belonged to a family that reckoned among its
members several princes of Memphis and high
priests of Ptah. She was born in the ninth year
of the reign of Ptolemy XIII, about 71 B.C., and
when fourteen years old she was married to her
half-brother, the priest P-Shere-en-Ptah.[3] During the first twelve years of her married life she

[1] This is an interesting reference to the use of an amulet,
which was a figure or ornament possessing magical power
and worn as a preservative against sickness or misfortune.

Amulets associated with Imhotep are not frequently met
with. Fig. xvii represents a specimen preserved in the
Egyptological Museum of the Liverpool University.

[2] British Museum, Egyptian Sculpture Gallery, Bay 29,
No. 1027. Cf. E. A. Budge, *Guide to the Egyptian Collec-
tions in the British Museum*, 1909, p. 274.

[3] His stela is also in the British Museum, Egyptian Sculpture Gallery, Bay 27, No. 1026.

XVII. AMULET OF IMHOTEP

gave birth to three daughters, but had no son, which caused her husband great grief. She and her husband prayed to the god Imhotep, the son of Ptah, for a son ; in response, the god, appearing to P-Shere-en-Ptah in a dream, promised to grant his prayer provided that he carried out certain works in connexion with the temple. When the priest awoke, he caused the works to be taken in hand, and soon after they were completed his wife gave birth to a son who was named Imhotep, and surnamed Pedi-Bast.[1]

Incubation sleep [2] in the temples was resorted to for many forms of sickness, suggestive intimations being given by the deity during natural or drug-produced dreams and interpreted by the priests. Doubtless in many cases a cure was effected through the awakening of an expectation of cure in the sleeper himself. Thus the temple-sleep was used as a form of faith-healing. Suggestions received during dreams that a cure had been effected were found to have achieved their

[1] British Museum, l. c., Bay 27, No. 1030.

[2] Incubation was by no means confined to the shrines of Imhotep. For example, at the temple of Medinet Habu night oracles were received through incubation from Thoth who was wont to descend on the temple each night in the form of an ibis. P. Boynan, *Thoth the Hermes of Egypt*, 1922, p. 168. Cf. also G. Foucart, on ' Dreams and Incubation ' in the *Encyclopaedia of Religion and Ethics*, v, p. 34.

purpose when the sufferer awoke.[1]   The more emotional and highly strung the patient, the greater the probability of cure.

As the centuries rolled by, the worship of Imhotep spread more and more widely, until eventually he became recognized all over Egypt as the god of medicine.   Indeed the learned magician-physician of the time of King Zoser became one of the most popular deities, as we learn from the eulogistic appreciations that have been handed down to us.   Thus he is described as ' the good physician of gods and men, a kind and merciful god, assuaging the sufferings of those in pain, healing the diseases of men and giving peaceful sleep to the restless and suffering '. Elsewhere he is spoken of as ' the god who protects human beings, who gives to him who calls upon him, who gives life to men and women, and who gives life to all who are bounden to him '.   At other times he is described as the ' god who looks after the sick ' and ' the worshipful or holy god who gives a son to him who has none '.

Another fine testimony says that he visits the

---

[1] Incubation dreams were also used for propaganda, devotees being urged to build further temples and spread the cult of the deity.   Priests also appeared during the night, apart from dreams, and, acting on behalf of the deity, indicated the path to recovery.   W. Schubart, *Ägypten von Alexander dem Grossen bis auf Mohammed*, 1892, pp. 314 ff.

suffering ' to give them peaceful sleep and heal their pains and diseases '.[1] The popularity of Imhotep will cause no surprise, since he both healed the sick, protected from accident and gave children to those who had hitherto been sterile. As Breasted has well said :

' The great wise man Imhotep was one of King Zoser's chief advisers. In priestly wisdom, in magic, in the formulation of wise proverbs, in medicine, in architecture, this remarkable figure of Zoser's reign left so notable a reputation that his name was never forgotten. The people sang of his proverbs centuries later, and 2,500 years after his death he had become a god of medicine whom the Greeks, who called him Imouthes, identified with their own Aesculapius.' [2]

In fact during the Hellenistic period the sage Imhotep, now deified, appears to have become the principal god worshipped at Memphis, and to have wellnigh superseded Ptah.

[1] Brugsch says that after recovery the patients used to dedicate to the god a model of the diseased member, such as an eye, an ear, a foot, &c. Brugsch, *Religion und Mythologie der alten Aegypter*, p. 527. Some specimens of Egyptian votive offerings in wood, bronze, and blue glazed ware may be seen in museums of Egyptology.

[2] Breasted, *A History of Egypt*, 1919, p. 113. Just as the Greeks identified Imhotep with their own deity of medicine, i. e. Asklepios, so the Egyptians also equated him with Eshmun, the Phoenician god of healing. Cf. W. A. Jayne, *The Healing Gods of Ancient Civilizations*, 1925, p. 138.

But apart from the temples specially associated with him, Imhotep was also worshipped in various other temples. Amongst them is the temple of Deir-el-Bahari where the Ptolemaic Chamber [1] was dedicated to two men who had both been deified, Imhotep the son of Ptah and Amenophis the son of Hapi.[2] On the wall of this Chamber is a fine representation of the deity Imhotep carrying a sceptre in his right hand and an ankh in his left. Close to the god is the inscription : ' I have given thee life combined with health and protection. I am thy protector.'

Other inscriptions describe Imhotep as ' the great Kheri-heb, the first chief one of the Ibis, Imhotep, the son of Ptah, south of his Wall, who listens to him who implores him, on the Western side of Thebes, who does good to its inhabitants, giving life, strength and joy to its dwellers, and enriching the land '. Behind the picture of Imhotep is a goddess having some resemblance to Hathor. Naville suggests that this figure is the mother of Imhotep who has also been deified and says : ' I give thee life ; I join to it health ; my protective power, Imhotep, is guarding thee.'

[1] This chamber dates from about 140 B.C., in the reign of Ptolemy IX Euergetes II.

[2] E. Naville, *The Temple of Deir-el-Bahari*, 1906, Part V, p. 11 and Pl. CXLIX.

Another shrine in which Imhotep was worshipped was the temple of Ptah at Thebes.[1] This temple was built by Tuthmosis III and restored by several of the Ptolemies. Here were worshipped Ptah, his wife Sekhmet, and their son Imhotep, together with Amenophis the son of Hapi.[2]

Another small Ptolemaic temple known at the present day as the Qasr-el-Agouz (Kasr el-Agouz) was erected by Euergetes II to the god Thoth. In the second hall may be seen the King sacrificing to Thoth, Imhotep, and the deified sage Amenophis. This temple stands south-west of the Colossi of Memnon.[3]

Yet another temple in which Imhotep and Amenophis were jointly worshipped was Medinet Habu, lying directly west of the Colossi.[4] Evidently the two famous sages of Egypt who had both been accorded divine honours were often worshipped in the same shrines.

The same applies to the temple of Deir el Medineh, which lies north-west of the Colossi.

---

[1] Baedeker's *Egypt*, 1914, p. 277; Plan of Karnak, p. 264.

[2] G. Maspero, *Ancient Sites and Modern Scenes*, pp. 444-5. Pictures of Ptah and Imhotep are sculptured on the walls of the temple.

[3] Baedeker's *Egypt*, 1914, p. 330, Plan, p. 280.

[4] Ibid., p. 330.

This temple was originally the grave of Amenophis and was converted by Ptolemy IV into
a shrine to the gods of the dead.[1] In it both he
and Imhotep were worshipped in company with
the full gods of Egypt.[2]

Apart from these public temples there appear
to have been in Ptolemaic times many small
shrines or altars which individuals erected in
their own homes in honour of their tutelary deity
Imhotep and in the hope of securing his protection against all sorts of misfortunes. In other
cases such shrines were hired out by their owners
in return for money payments contributed by
sick persons or such as needed some oracular
guidance in a difficulty. Such shrines were
dedicated both to Isis and Asklepios (*sc.* Imhotep),
the latter, however, being the principal god of
healing.[3]

The interesting discovery has recently been
made that under the Ptolemies regular festivals
were celebrated in honour of the god Imhotep
in much the same way as was done in the case

[1] A. Erman, *A Handbook of the Egyptian Religion*, p.
175.

[2] In several of these temples may be seen some of the mural
reliefs of Imhotep mentioned in Appendix E.

[3] W. Schubart, *Ägypten von Alexander dem Grossen bis auf
Mohammed*, 1922, p. 300.

of other traditional deities.[1] It is well known
that festivals and fasts played a leading part in
the religious life of the Egyptians and were
celebrated with vociferous demonstrations of
joy—processions accompanied by banners, singing,
dancing, and sacred emblems. Pilgrimages and
banquets also formed part of the festival, which
might extend over several days or even weeks.[2]
Doubtless in the case of Imhotep there would
be abundant expressions of gratitude by his
former patients for the wonderful cures he had
performed.

This discovery has been made by means of an
inscription on the recently found carved pedestal
of a lost statue, now in the British Museum.[3]
The inscription begins with an address to his
lord Imhotep, son of Ptah, from his divine friend,
the prophet and scribe Pedi-Bast : ' I am thy
son, perfect in the service of thy *Ka* on all thy
festival days, at the commencement of the
seasons and on all festivals taken together.'

[1] H. Gauthier, ' Un Nouveau Monument du Dieu Imhotep ', *Bulletin de l'Institut Français d'Archéologie Orientale*,
1918, xiv (i), p. 33.

[2] For further details compare the article by Foucart,
' Festivals and Fasts ', in *Encyclopaedia of Religion and Ethics*,
v, p. 853. Cf. also *Z. f. Ägyptische Sprache*, 1886, xxiv,
pp. 20, 24–5.

[3] Southern Egyptian Sculpture Gallery, Bay 29, No. 347.

There were six festivals in all, celebrated on the following dates : [1]

Day of Festival	Egyptian Month	Date
16th day 3rd month of spring.	Epiphi.	31st May.
11th day 2nd month of winter.	Mekhir.	27th Dec.
9th day 4th month of spring.	Mesoré.	23rd June.
17th day 4th month of Shemu.	Mesoré.	1st July.
23rd day 4th month of Shemu.	Mesoré.	7th July.
4th day 2nd month of Shemu.	Paoni.	19th April.

It will be observed these festivals are not arranged in the chronological order of the months of the year ; their order corresponds to certain events in the life of the god Imhotep which they are intended to commemorate.

A. First festival.

> ' The day on which was born Imhotep of his father Ptah and his mother Khreduonkh ; the heart of the great god, the father of the gods, is pleased at seeing him.'

B. Second festival.

> ' The day of the first festival of Imhotep ;

[1] H. Brugsch, *Matériaux pour le Calendrier des Anciens Égyptiens*, p. 80.

he appears before his father Ptah and Sekhmet, the great one, beloved of Ptah. She ordains . . . and glorifies his image.'

C. Third festival.

' The day of the slaying of the vile Asiatics by Sekhmet, the great one, beloved of Ptah. She tears off their limbs whilst burning them. She capsizes their boats in the region of the land of the Red Lake.'

D. Fourth festival.

' The day of lamentation of his father Ptah for Imhotep when he (?) died . . . his body . . . his spirit when it was re-united (?) ' (probably an allusion to the separation of spirit and body at the moment of the death of the god).

E. Fifth festival.

' The day on which Imhotep reposes before his father after his death : he enters and goes out before the great god : the re-union of his spirit with his body takes place and he rests in the great Dehan, a cavern dear to his heart.'

F. Sixth festival.

' The day on which the spirit of Imhotep departs towards the great place of sojourn of this god upon the whole earth.'

No doubt at these festivals the Imhotepian

devotees would bring their offerings to the
sanctuary, some of them being given as thank-
offerings for recovery from illness or accident,
others in anticipation of such benefits in future
years.[1]

Some interesting details have survived of the
allowances made to the priests who were associated
with the Egyptian temples during the second
century B.C.[2] These allowances, known as
the συντάξεις σιτικαί, appear to have consisted
of wine, milk, oil, and bread ; the two forms of
oil were sesame and kiki (i. e. castor) oil,[3] while
the loaves were made of spelt, i. e. a form of wheat
(*Triticum spelta*).

At the Asklepieion at Memphis, in addition to
the ordinary priests, a form of lower priesthood
seems to have been in existence, represented by
the so-called twin-sisters (δίδυμαι). These twin-
sisters (ἱερόδουλοι) received daily for their services

---

[1] In the Cairo Museum is preserved a θησαυρός or money-
box, derived from the temple of Asklepios and Hygieia at
Ptolemais, and intended to receive donations from worshippers.
Such money-boxes were commonly used in Egyptian temples
of the Graeco-Roman period ; the Cairo specimen is sur-
mounted by a serpent's head, doubtless as a symbol. *Z. f.
Ägyptische Sprache*, 1902–3, xl, p. 140.

[2] W. Otto, *Priester und Tempel im Hellenistischen Ägypten*,
1908, i, pp. 117, 373.

[3] This was the *Ricinus communis*, a common plant in
Egypt. Rawlinson, *History of Herodotus*, ii. 94.

at the Asklepieion [1] four loaves a day, called cyllêstis (κύλλαστις).

On what grounds did Imhotep receive the very rare honour of being raised to the full rank of divinity? Only a few other instances in which an ordinary mortal receives apotheosis are known in the whole of Egyptian history.[2] During his life King Zoser bestowed on him the highest office in the State, that of vizier; but posterity conferred an even greater honour when it placed him among the deities of Egypt.

Maspero[3] attributes this signal favour to the cumulative qualifications of architect, physician, sage, and magician, but attributes the apotheosis mainly to his skill in magic. 'It is', he says, 'in virtue of his powers as a magician that Imhotep was deified.'

There can be no question that in Egypt magic exerted an enormous influence in the life both of the individual and of the nation. It was invoked

[1] Rawlinson, *History of Herodotus*, ii. 77.

[2] This of course does not apply to the Pharaohs, since these were never looked upon as ordinary mortals. Sethe enumerates eight instances of the deification of individuals not of royal rank. Cf. *Encyclopaedia of Religion and Ethics*, vi, p. 650.

[3] G. Maspero, *Études de Mythologie et d'Archéologie Égyptiennes*, 1916, viii, p. 134. Cf. also his article on the deification of Amenophis: 'How an Egyptian Statesman became a God', in *New Light on Ancient Egypt*, 1908, p. 189.

in all questions of life and death, of love and hatred, of health and sickness. But this potent influence does not prevent the reputation of Imhotep being also due to exceptional skill in the use of the rich *materia medica* at his disposal, for it must have been chiefly in psycho-neuroses that magic was successful. Physical as well as psychical therapeutics may well have been used in co-operation, and by combining their forces have raised him to a position of rare eminence. Doubtless after his death his reputation led to pilgrimages to his tomb, when incubation sleep in his adjoining temple was followed by many recoveries. Every successful cure would confirm the public confidence that the former magician-physician still possessed superhuman powers. Fame would grow into veneration and eventually into true worship.

The deification of Imhotep proves that the Egyptians believed it possible for gods to be evolved out of common mortals. Speaking generally, an ordinary individual was not supposed to have any right to immortality, but the part of him which persists and which is called his *Ka* or double might be kept alive, provided it was unceasingly nourished and comforted by actual bread, meat, and drink and other necessary supplies.

When the *Ka* of a deceased was thus supported
by his descendants or by devotees, the moment
of his dissolution could be indefinitely postponed.
Even the gods, although less perishable than
mortals, were subject to like infirmities as were
the latter, e. g. to disease, senility and death, and
needed liturgies and incantations as well as
material sustenance if their continued existence
was to be assured. Thus the difference between
a deity and an ordinary mortal was merely one
of degree. Provided therefore that the descendants of a deceased person continued to support
him by generous gifts and endowments in the
same manner as was done in the case of a god, his
continued existence would be assured. In Maspero's words, ' mortal men would have manu-
factured a new immortal '. The generous gifts
provided by his devotees would at the same time
enhance his prestige ; this prestige would bring
further gifts and thus increase his chances of
attaining immortality. Such seems to have been
the sequence of events which led to the apotheosis
of one who had originally been an ordinary man
of flesh and blood.

Long before the Greek conquest of Egypt by
Alexander, Imhotep had become generally recognized as the deity of medicine. The Greeks who
called him Imouthes amalgamated him with their

own Asklepios (Aesculapius), so that for some centuries the Egyptian deity of medicine may be described as in some measure a fusion of the ancient Imhotep and the much more modern Asklepios. Frequently, indeed, the identity of Imhotep is concealed under the name Asklepios.[1]

During the Ptolemaic period there seems to have been some relation between the worship of Imhotep and that of the sacred bull of Ptah named Apis. Ammianus Marcellinus, referring to the time of Julius Augustus (63 B.C.–A.D. 14), thus describes the association of Apis with the temple of Imhotep at Memphis. When the Apis bull had died, ' another is sought amid great public mourning ; and if one can be found distinguished by all the required marks, he is led to Memphis, a city of great renown, and especially celebrated for the patronage of the god Aesculapius. And after he has been led into the city by one hundred priests and conducted into a chamber, he is looked upon as consecrated and is said to point out by evident means the signs of future events. Some also of those who come to him he repels by un-favourable signs ; as it is reported he formally rejected Caesar Germanicus when he offered him

[1] Imhotep was also at times assimilated with other deities that were associated with him, e. g. Harpokrates in Thebes, and Khnum in Elephantine. Pauly, *Real-Encyclopädie*, ix (ii), col. 1217.

food ; thus portending what shortly happened.'[1]
Doubtless Apis was taken into the inner sanctum
of Asklepios (*sc.* Imhotep) in order that he might
be touched and thus consecrated by the statue
of the deity.

An interesting question arises as to how late
the worship of Imhotep lasted on during the
Christian era. The palaeography of the *graffiti*
at the sanatorium at Deir-el-Bahari which relate
to Imhotep indicates that they probably belong
to the second century A. D., but not much beyond
it.[2] There was, however, a special local reason
for their discontinuance. The raids of the bar-
barian tribes of Nubia in the middle of the third
century would doubtless interfere with security
of life, frighten away invalids, and check pilgrimages to the shrine. Probably, therefore, Deir-el-
Bahari ceased to be a health resort for the Greeks
and Romans soon after A. D. 200.

In the north of Egypt, on the other hand, there
is evidence that the worship of Imhotep continued
considerably later, and indeed that his reputation
as the deity of medicine gradually grew in com-
parison with that of the other Egyptian gods,
until in the fourth century he had come to be

[1] Ammianus Marcellinus, tr. by C. D. Yonge, xxii, 14,
p. 306.
[2] Milne, *J. of Egyptian Archaeology*, 1914, i, p. 98.

regarded as the leading divinity of Memphis.[1] As
Otto says : ' It is very remarkable that the
deified Imhotep, who was probably not acknowledged as a god until the Saite period, and did not
receive his fullest recognition as god till the
Ptolemaic period, by the time of Ammianus
Marcellinus [2] had come to be the chief deity of
Memphis.' [3] Thus his worship evidently extended well into the Roman period, to the time
when profound changes had taken place in the
internal and external economy of Egypt. The
country in fact had become part of a new world.
Her glorious history—one of the most momentous
epochs in the history of man—had closed, and
she was living an artificial life in which she no
longer played an active part.

The collapse of ancient Egyptian civilization
was due to a variety of causes acting cumulatively.
One of these causes was the passing of the country
under the guardianship of Rome in the year
30 B.C. Henceforth she became a vassal of the
Roman Empire and was governed by its represen-

[1] Imhotep appears still to have retained his reputation as
a patron of magic, as the alchemist Zosimos (3rd c. A.D.)
entitled one of his works Ἰμούθ, i. e. Imhotep. Pauly, *Real-
Encyclopädie*, ix (ii), col. 1217.

[2] Ammianus Marcellinus lived *ca.* A.D. 330–400.

[3] W. Otto, *Priester und Tempel im Hellenistischen Ägypten*,
1908, ii, p. 214.

tative. The steady drain involved by the annual tribute of corn to feed the hungry Romans, combined with the extortions of her governors, depleted the supply of capital wealth. The bucolic rebellion of A. D. 172 was a symptom of the national distress and aggravated the exhaustion of the country. From this period down to about A. D. 300 the land became more and more impoverished.

Another potent influence at work in the disintegration of the ancient régime was the spread of Christianity, whose doctrines were well established in Alexandria in the second century and were gradually being diffused throughout the country. In spite of persecutions the number of churches steadily grew, so that by about A. D. 300 many towns on the Nile were provided with places of Christian worship. The conversion of the Emperor Constantine (*ca.* A. D. 288 to 337) to Christianity gave a further impetus to the new religion and caused many worshippers of the gods of Egypt to transfer their devotion to an austere form of Christianity. Indeed, during the next two centuries these converts did their best to root out the native forms of worship. Meanwhile the national faith in the ancient deities had weakened almost to a vanishing point, and with that weakening the associated priesthood and

ritual would naturally disappear.[1] Associated
with the progress of Christianity was the growth
of Christian monasticism, which, while it had
sprung from Egyptian monasticism, had in course
of time become an important adjunct to the new
religion. These monasteries indeed frequently
occupied buildings that had previously been
Egyptian temples, and naturally brought all native
religious observances to an end. So numerous
had the monks become that in the fourth century
the Emperor Valens (A. D. 364–378) sent three
thousand troops into the desert of Nitria to compel
the able-bodied ascetics who had retired there to
enlist in the imperial armies. In that desert alone
there lived no less than five thousand monks.[2]

Further, a large amount of labour was withdrawn
by the monasteries from the economic resources of
the country and devoted to ecclesiastical purposes.
Thus, deprived of an important productive element in its population and drained of many of its

[1] W. Otto, *Priester und Tempel im Hellenistischen Ägypten*,
1908, ii, p. 214. Other references to the priests of Imhotep
(*sc.* Asklepios) during the early Christian era will be found in
Hieronymus, Vita S. Hilarionis, cap. 21 (Migne, *Patrol.
Latina*, xxiii, p. 38) ; Clement of Alexandria, *Strom.*, i,
cap. 21, 399.

An account of early Christianity in Egypt is given by
W. Scott, *Hermetica*, i, pp. 65 ff.

[2] E. Gibbon, *Decline and Fall of the Roman Empire*,
chaps. xxv and xxxvii.

material resources, the nation sank to a low economic level, so low indeed that the available capital was insufficient to support the miserably debased coinage. By A. D. 370 taxes were paid in kind and commerce was reduced to barter.

A third factor in the general disruption was the introduction of Greek culture and science, including Greek medicine. Ever since the founding of Alexandria in 331 B. C. Hellenic influences had gradually been permeating and undermining the ancient methods of treating the sick, based partly on experience and partly on magic, that had held sway for many centuries. The Egyptian magician-physicians had been content to use prescriptions that had been handed down for many generations, rarely testing their results by means of experiment, while, on the other hand, the patient was still encouraged in the old belief that the magic formulas which were recited, whenever a potion was swallowed, were able to placate the evil spirits that had caused the disease and were at least as potent as the physical remedy.

This antiquated procedure now gave way under the influence of a spirit of inquiry and experiment, rapid progress being made in anatomy, physiology, *materia medica*, and pathology.[1] The result was that the primitive system of medicine which had

[1] An excellent summary is given by E. A. Budge in his

been in vogue since the days of Imhotep passed
into oblivion, the old order changing and giving
place to new.

Lastly, amongst the forces which brought the
ancient civilization of Egypt to an end were the
hostile incursions into Egypt during the Roman
period. Both the Blemmyes of the Eastern
desert and the Nobadae of the Western desert
harassed the Roman conquerors at intervals during
the first three centuries of the Christian era, and
the Emperor Diocletian (284–305) was obliged
to put an end to their invasions by an annual
subsidy.

The story of the political and religious dis-
turbances that raged during these early centuries
of our era is too long and complex to be told
here ; suffice it to say that they combined to
render the foreign occupation a period of stress
and turmoil in which the constituent elements
of early Egyptian civilization broke asunder.
Indeed the final collapse of Egypt was largely
due to the purely military government of the

Introduction to the Syrian Anatomy, Pathology and Thera-
peutics, 1913, i, pp. xxxvii ff. Cf. also F. H. Garrison, *History*
of Medicine, 1921, p. 93 ; K. Sudhoff, *Studien z. Geschichte der*
Medizin (Puschmann-Stiftung), 1909, Nos. 5, 6. The first
great medical school of antiquity was established at Alexandria, where there were extensive laboratories, clinics and
libraries.

Romans, who did little to prevent the inroads of savages and allowed the country to lapse into barbarism. The Egyptian people had lost all desire for independence and did nothing to resist the oppressive alien government. Thus the Moslem conquest of the country in A.D. 639 became easy, and for over three centuries Egypt became a province of the Eastern Caliphate.

The worship of Imhotep at Memphis seems to have lingered on until the process of national dissolution was far advanced. Doubtless the traditions of his skill in the *ars medendi*, dating from the glorious days of the early Dynasties, kept alive the popular confidence in him, even when faith in many of the other deities had faded away. All through his long career since the days of the Pharaoh Zoser he played a worthy part on the stage of history; for ever will his name be held in grateful remembrance.

To Imhotep, indeed, may truthfully be applied the words of Virgil, written not many years before the Roman conquest of his country :

'Semper honos, nomenque tuum, laudesque manebunt.'

V

ANCIENT EGYPTIAN MEDICINE

A SHORT *excursus* may be permitted in order to indicate the extraordinary development of the healing art that had been reached by the time of Imhotep. The full story is a fascinating one, but it cannot be told here. With scarcely a trace of infancy, the *ars medica* suddenly emerges, exhibiting an unparalleled stage of evolution in Egypt when compared with any other country. In the words of Foucart : ' The Egyptian science of healing constituted from the very beginning a system several thousand years in advance of the rest of human society.' [1] At the same time medicine was closely interwoven with magic, each of these elements acting and reacting on the other. The briefest survey of what had been achieved in the Pyramid age must suffice.

It will be convenient in the first place to summarize the progress made in the *ars medendi*, and then to deal with the elements of magic and occultism which were closely interwoven with it.

[1] *Encyclopaedia of Religion and Ethics*, iv, p. 752.

Fortunately a considerable number of medical documents have survived written in the hieratic script on rolls of papyrus. The most important of these is the Ebers Papyrus [1] which was actually written in the early XVIIIth Dynasty, *ca.* 1550 B.C., but which was evidently compiled from one or more other books many centuries earlier. Indeed the document itself states that some portions date from the Ist Dynasty,[2] and therefore were in part at least in existence during Imhotep's lifetime. The Papyrus contains a long list of prescriptions for numerous named ailments and specifies the remedies to be used, as well as their doses and the mode of administration. Evidently considerable progress had been made, especially in clinical examination, diagnosis and therapeutics. Further, there was an accurate knowledge of the skeleton and of the method of treating fractures successfully. The position and

[1] The other important medical papyri are the Hearst Papyrus about as ancient as the Ebers, the Berlin Medical Papyrus written somewhat later, the Kahun Medical Papyrus, which is surely of the XIIth Dynasty, i. e. considerably earlier than the Ebers, the London Medical Papyrus, the Edwin Smith Papyrus, and another papyrus at Berlin, which contains a collection of spells and prescriptions for mothers and their babies.

[2] For an excellent *résumé* of the subject cf. W. R. Dawson's paper ' Medicine and Surgery in Ancient Egypt ', *New York Medical Times*, Feb. 1925.

function of the stomach and intestines were known, as well as the fact that the great blood-vessels run from the heart to every part of the body. Some of the glosses in the Edwin Smith Papyrus reveal an acquaintance with anatomy which could only have been acquired by dissection.[1]

In the Ebers Papyrus lengthy descriptions are given of the vascular system, and the widespread influence of a disordered cardiac action is recognized, the heart being described as ' the beginning of all the members '.[2] There is also some inkling of a circulation of the blood ; pulsation was perceived although the actual pumping action of the heart was not understood. On the other hand, the relation of the pulse to the heart was well recognized. Thus the Papyrus says : ' When the heart is diseased its work is imperfectly performed : the vessels proceeding from the heart become inactive, so that you cannot feel them ; they become full of air and water.' This latter statement is explained by the belief that the arteries contained air instead of

[1] J. H. Breasted, *Recueil Champollion*, 1922, p. 425.
[2] Papyrus Ebers, 99, 1. W. Max Müller discovered some pictures which he believed to represent surgical operations (2500 B. C.). *Egyptological Researches*, Carnegie Institution, Washington, 1906. Cf. also Walsh, *J. American Med. Ass.*, xlix, pp. 1593–5.

blood, an erroneous conclusion based on the condition observed at post-mortems.

The conception of air reaching to every part of the body was familiar, although the air was supposed to travel by the arteries. The breath when entering the nostrils was believed to penetrate to the heart and internal organs, and to supply the whole blood abundantly.

Surgery was not highly developed. The knife and cautery were familiar, and simple operations were regularly performed on the head, neck and extremities, although surgeons never went so far as to open the abdomen. Fractures were treated with splints made of fibre, and many observations on mummies show that union with but little displacement was secured. More complicated operations were performed on the domestic animals than on man.

The custom of mummification, although not connected with medicine either in purpose or practice, exercised a profound influence on the growth of that science. Not only did the opening of the abdomen and the removal of the viscera familiarize the Egyptians with the form and position of many internal organs, but it reconciled the people of Egypt for more than thirty centuries to the idea of cutting the dead human body. Thus it overcame the popular prejudice against systematic dissection which prevented Greek physicians from acquiring a knowledge of practical anatomy in their own country.

It is, however, in the realms of diagnosis and therapeutics that the most astounding advance had been made, indicating a real interest in disease. Knowledge was admittedly empiric, but the accumulated experience of remedies employed during many centuries had borne rich fruit. At least 15 distinct diseases of the abdomen, 11 of the bladder, 10 of the rectum and anus, 29 of the eyes, 6 of the ears, 18 of the skin were diagnosed and treated on definite principles. From the symptoms described in the papyri about 250 different kinds of disease can be differentiated. Evidently the physicians who practised on the banks of the Nile possessed in some measure the scientific spirit, were capable of accurate clinical observations, and competent to co-ordinate and interpret symptoms. In fact so minute a classification of disease implies considerable scientific advance.

Herodotus in the following quotation refers to the prevalence of specialism as a feature of Egyptian medicine : ' The art of medicine is thus divided : each physician applies himself to one disease only, and not more. All places abound in physicians ; some are for the eyes, others for the head, others for the teeth, others for the intestines, and others for internal disorders.'[1] Recently discovered medical papyri, however, throw considerable doubt on such specialism, every part of medicine being apparently practised by physicians. Moreover, the Westcar Papyrus indicates that midwifery was not regarded as a department of medicine as was formerly believed.[2] Veterinary medicine was not overlooked, and a papyrus (that of Kahun) devoted to that branch of the healing art has survived. Further evidence of the advanced state of Egyptian medicine may be found in the extensive *materia medica* which formed the *armamentarium medici*.

The Edwin Smith Papyrus also reveals to us that there were in early Egypt medical practitioners who carried out dissection of the human body, organized their observations, and based conclusions on facts they had observed. Evidently they acted on the principle *nec silet mors*. A large number of the drugs used several millennia ago still figure in modern Pharmacopoeias. The flora of Egypt was rich in medicinal herbs, as Homer

[1] Herodotus, ii. 84. The passages of medical interest in Herodotus have been collected by W. R. Dawson. Cf. *Annals of Medical History*, 1924, vi, No. 3, pp. 183 ff.

[2] G. Maspero, *Popular Stories of Ancient Egypt*, 1916, pp. 36 ff.

points out,[1] and evidently their therapeutic pro-
perties were carefully studied and utilized.

Amongst vegetable products frequently mentioned are castor oil, opium, aloes, coriander, cara-
way, gentian, turpentine, myrrh, juniper, fennel,
henbane, linseed and peppermint ; but recent
research throws much doubt, at least in some
cases, on their correct identification. On the
other hand, iron, soda, lime, salts of lead, sulphate
of copper, magnesia were certainly amongst the
mineral products in use. Other drugs were
derived from the animal body, such as gall and
blood from the ox, lion and hippopotamus, as well
as fats from these and other animals ; even
coprotherapy was common.[2] It is interesting to
observe that the use of the secretions and parts
of the animal body as remedies, now a worldwide practice, was first introduced by Egyptian
physicians.[3]

[1] ' Earth the grain-giver yields herbs in the greatest plenty,
many that are healing in the cup, and many baneful.'

[2] Many such fanciful remedies were prescribed in this
country so recently as the seventeenth century and even later.
Cf. the Pharmacopoeia of the Royal College of Physicians of
London, A.D. 1651.

[3] According to Osler the use of magic and of the secretions
and parts of the animal body as remedies form two worldwide methods of practice that found their earliest illustrations
in ancient Egypt. W. Osler, *The Evolution of Modern Medicine*, p. 13.

It is pleasant to think that even in those far-off days opium was used to relieve poor suffering humanity, and Pliny states that among the herbs given to Helen of Troy was nepenthes, which caused ' oblivion of sorrow '.

Even the forms in which remedies were administered showed some clinical insight into pathological processes. Gargles, salves, lozenges, inhalations, snuffs, suppositories, pills, capsules, enemata, fumigations, poultices and plasters were all employed. Ingredients were added for the purpose of disguising nauseous drugs.

The large number of remedies and prescriptions mentioned in the Ebers Papyrus prove conclusively that therapeutics were carefully studied. The same Papyrus shows that remedies were classified into special groups, amongst which were sedatives, narcotics, hypnotics, antispasmodics, mydriatics, myotics, expectorants, tonics, emetics, carminatives, purgatives, astringents, cholagogues, anthelmintics, diuretics, diaphoretics, emmenagogues, oxytocics, galactagogues, haemostatics, emollients, disinfectants, antidotes, and so forth. In brief, while scientific medicine was still in its infancy, empiric therapeutics were highly advanced.

No sketch of the Egyptian knowledge of medicine, however, is complete without reference to the prevailing faith in magic. Magic was the mother of medicine and never ceased to influence its offspring. In fact any eulogy of Egyptian therapeutics is heavily discounted when the ever-present accompaniment of magical formulas, amulets and incantations is taken into consideration. Disease was generally attributed, not to a disturbance of normal functions, but to a malign spirit or god who had entered the body and attacked it furiously. Unless this evil spirit could be expelled before irreparable damage had been done, recovery was hopeless. The evil spirits or demons insinuated themselves into the individual by the nostrils, mouth or ears, and once inside devoured his vital substance. The character and termination of the resulting disease depended on the progress made in the destructive activity of the invading spirit, its virulence depending also on times and seasons of the year, on lucky and unlucky days and similar contingencies. The physician-priest-magician who treats the sick person must first of all discover the nature and if possible the name of the evil spirit in possession, and then seek to expel it by every means in his power. He must be expert in magic, knowing suitable incantations, and skilful in making amulets adapted to the occasion. As opportunity presents he must resort to invocations and impressive ritual. Material remedies must also be tried, and recourse had to the rich pharmacopoeia which the experience of centuries had accumulated. The best practitioners were in some measure rationalistic, and carefully diagnosed between those cases for which magic and exorcisms were most suited, those for which incubation in the temple promised the best results, and those which called for incantations accompanied by drugs.[1]

The following is a specimen of an incantation which had to be recited during the preparation of a medicine in order to endow it with the right power : ' That Isis might make free, make free. That Isis might make Horus free from all evil that his brother Set had done to him when he slew his father Osiris. O Isis, great enchantress, free me, release me from all evil red things, from the fever of the god and the fever of the goddess, from death, and death from pain, and the pain which comes over me ; as thou hast freed, as thou hast released thy son Horus, whilst I enter into the fire and go forth from the water ', &c.[2]

A different formula was recited as the invalid swallowed his dose : ' Welcome, remedy, welcome, which destroyest the trouble in this my

[1] G. Maspero, *Life in Ancient Egypt and Assyria*, p. 119.
[2] Papyrus Ebers, i. 12 ff.

heart and in these my limbs. The magic of Horus is victorious in the remedy.'[1]

Another common magical practice was to write down an incantation on papyrus, to wash it off into the medicine, and then to administer the latter to the patient, as is still commonly done in Eastern countries.[2] Instead of such a simple phrase as ' Prescription for curing such a disease ' the expression ' Prescription for expelling or terrifying such a disease ' would be adopted, with the evident implication of demoniacal possession.

This view of the nature of disease naturally had a fundamental and blighting influence on therapeutics. Disease caused by the pernicious influence of an indwelling spirit must be combated by magic, incantations and spells, although remedies might also relieve symptoms and abolish pain. Rational therapeutics and magic were thus closely interwoven in the practice of the magician-physician, who had to distinguish between diseases curable by drugs and those requiring psycho-therapy. In the early days superstitious and sacerdotal measures probably predominated, while as time passed on exact observation and thera-peutics more and more gained the upper hand, sorcery yielding to science. The choice between

[1] Papyrus Ebers, ii. 1–2.
[2] W. Max Müller, *Egyptian Mythology*, p. 199.

theurgical or rational methods of treatment would also largely depend on the philosophical views of the physician, and we have evidence that much less magic was used in some cases than in others. Probably magic ceremonies were resorted to as a last resource when the skill of the physician was baffled. The *malade imaginaire* was doubtless as common a phenomenon as he is to-day ; many faith cures took place at famous shrines.

It may seem strange that such an apparently absurd occult force as magic retained a potent influence through all the centuries of ancient Egyptian history. On the other hand, it must be remembered that sick persons, even if they belong to the educated class, have some excuse for fantastic actions and beliefs. They are abnormally emotional and suggestible, and readily clutch at any remedy, even if irrational, that presents itself, especially if powerfully supported by tradition and authority. As is well known, the benefits conferred by medicaments depend largely on the confidence felt in the physician and in his prescriptions.

We cannot doubt that Imhotep, with his wide outlook on life, his experience of men and human affairs, and his interest in astronomy and other sciences, inclined to the side of scientific medicine. Indeed, as Erman says, ' the son of the goddess

Sechmet, the demigod Imhôtep, was in later times considered to be the creator of medical knowledge '.[1]

HYGIENE

The advanced state of hygiene also proves a high stage of civilization. The Egyptians boasted that they were the healthiest of all mortals, and regulated the sanitation of the town, of the dwelling, and even of the person, while the priests set up a high standard of cleanliness by their frequent ablutions and the immaculate purity of their clothing.[2] The homes of the people were fumigated from time to time to keep them sweet, suitable precautions being taken to prevent the annoyance of wasps and mosquitoes. There was also some knowledge of antiseptics, since the virtues of extreme dryness and of certain chemicals like nitre, common salt and alcohol as preservatives were recognized. Evidently the importance of sanitation was well understood. Even in those far-off days experience had taught the lesson that ὑγιαίνειν ἄριστον ἐστίν. The value of preventive medicine was also well recognized. The Egyp-

---

[1] A. Erman, *Life in Ancient Egypt*, p. 357.

[2] In order to preserve their purity of body, the priests washed themselves from head to foot in cold water twice every day and twice every night.

tians probably knew that the majority of diseases proceed from indigestion and excess of eating, and these evils they avoided or combated by frequent days of abstinence, by emetics, gentle aperients, and other means of relieving the system. The superiority of prophylaxis as compared with therapeutics was evidently appreciated. ' The whole manner of life ', says Diodorus, ' was so evenly ordered that it would appear as though it had been arranged according to the rules of health by a learned physician, rather than by a law-giver.'

These few facts will suffice to indicate in outline the extraordinary interest that was taken in remedies in ancient Egypt, and the progress that had been made. But it cannot be claimed that Egyptian medicine ever developed into a scientific system. Rather should its stage be described as one in which superstition and science struggled for mastery. Which indeed of us can say that this perennial conflict has, even to-day, been finally won by either combatant ?

VI

HONOUR TO WHOM HONOUR IS DUE

STRANGE it is that the claims of Imhotep to be recognized as the tutelary deity of medicine have been so neglected. Many centuries before the exodus of the Israelites from Egypt,[1] long before the recognition of Asklepios by the Greeks as their legendary god of medicine,[2] long before the days of Homer,[3] long before the birth of Hippocrates,[4] there lived in Egypt a magician-physician so famous for his skill in healing disease that he became recognized eventually as the Egyptian god of medicine. To him surely belongs the highest place in our hagiology ; to him should physicians all the world over look up

[1] The Exodus from Egypt is believed to have taken place *ca.* 1230 B.C. Cf. *Encyclopaedia Britannica*, iii, p. 868.

[2] The cult of Asklepios appears not to go back farther than the time of Homer when Asklepios was still but a Thessalian hero and clever leech, and the father of two heroes, Machaon and Podaleirus, who fought before Troy and became famous physicians. And yet on the strength of such a trivial claim Asklepios has been for centuries our emblematic god of medicine, the reputed healer of men. His figure appears in countless diplomas, coins and seals associated with hospitals and medical societies in every civilized country.

[3] *Ca.* 850 B.C.   [4] *Ca.* 460 B.C.

as the patron spirit of the *ars medendi*, as the emblematic god of medicine.

The reason for the neglect of Imhotep doubtless lies in the fact that it is only since Champollion deciphered the hieroglyphs about a century ago that the civilization of ancient Egypt has become known to the learned world ; until then all contemporary records, whether depicted in the temples or tombs, or inscribed on papyri, were undecipherable. Meanwhile Greek and Roman scholarship had for many centuries been familiar, with the result that the mythological lore relating to the classical deity of the healing art has become interwoven with the history of medicine in all civilized countries to the exclusion of the much older Egyptian deities.

Surely the time has come to do justice to the venerable figure described in the above pages, and to elevate Imhotep to the place of honour which is his due.[1]

---

[1] The Reading Pathological Society, the oldest Pathological Society in the United Kingdom, has recently adopted Imhotep, the Egyptian deity of medicine, as its Badge. This Badge shows the figure of the god executed in blue enamel and enclosed in a gold frame, and was presented to the Society by Sir Stewart Abram, as a souvenir of his Presidency. This is probably the first recognition by a Medical Society of the claims of Imhotep to be recognized as the patron spirit of the healing art.

THE EPILOGUE

WE have now completed the story of the venerable physician, whom Sir W. Osler calls 'Dr.' Imhotep, from the time of his dramatic appearance as vizier and magician-physician of King Zoser to his elevation to the rank of one of the full Egyptian deities. The contemplation of a career so varied in its pursuits, so notable in its achievements, so trusted by suffering humanity, so glorified in its final apotheosis must call forth a tribute of admiration. The worship of Imhotep extended well into the Roman period, at any rate as late as the fourth century of our era, so that his career, one of unique interest, extends over a period of about three thousand years. His name deserves to be held in everlasting remembrance as one of the few men of genius recorded in the history of ancient Egypt ; he is one of the fixed stars in the Egyptian firmament. His influence still remained dominant when the Egyptian civilization had long passed its meridian, and the country had become the vassal first of Greece and eventually of Rome. The *graffiti* of the rich Greeks and Romans who visited the ruined

temples and tombs still record the homage paid
to our hero and the widespread faith in his power
to heal the sick devotees who flocked to his
shrines.

During the Greek and Roman periods of
Egyptian history, Imhotep, *alias* Imouthes, became more and more closely identified with
Asklepios or Aesculapius the Greek and after-
wards the Roman god of medicine. Ultimately
indeed Imhotep was entirely merged in the latter
deity.[1]

In Egypt, as everywhere else, ' the old order
changeth, giving place to new.' In the course
of the intervening centuries time's eroding finger
and the vandalism of man have wrought strange
transformations in the temples where the beloved
Imhotep formerly reigned as the beneficent deity
who gave life and health to the sick and suffering.
His chief temple at Memphis is now a scene of
desolation. Where once the sacred aisles and
pillars echoed to the march of priest and worshipper, all is silence, save for bats and owls
and scarabs. The impressive ceremonial, the
magic rites and incantations that ministered to
the healing art have ceased for ever.

No longer do the seekers after health crave
permission to sleep within the precincts of his

[1] *Encyclopaedia Britannica*, xxiv, p. 681.

temple in the hope that the deity would appear to them in dreams and reveal the panacea for their sickness. No longer do devoted patients sing and dance before his shrine with hearts bursting with gratitude for a new lease of health and life.

The smaller sanctuary at Philae is submerged in a vast reservoir destined to bring material blessings to the country in lieu of the healing virtues formerly associated with the temple. The glory has also departed from the other shrines linked with Imhotep's worship which have been alluded to above.

Let us, however, be thankful that even to this day there survive some material and visible memorials of the immortal Egyptian physician. The terraced Pyramid of Sakkarah, the ruins at Philae, at Deir-el-Bahari and elsewhere will long remain as imposing *reliquiae* recalling the part he played on the stage of history ; and even when pyramid and temple have crumbled into dust his name will still be held in undying remembrance. Deep are the footprints he has left on the sands of time, and physicians all over the world will ever revere him as one of the pioneers of their ancient profession, as one whose name ' on fame's eternall beade-roll is worthie to be fyled '. *Medice immortalis, in perpetuum ave !*

APPENDIXES

A. BIBLIOGRAPHY [1]

BIRCH, S. 'Two Egyptian Tablets of the Ptolemaic Period.' *Archaeologia*, vol. xxxix.

BISSING, W. v. *Deutsche Literaturzeitung*, 1902, col. 2330.

BREASTED, J. H. *A History of Egypt*, 1909, p. 112.

British Museum Publications. *Guides to the Egyptian Galleries.**

BRUGSCH, H. *Religion und Mythologie der alten Aegypter*, 1890, p. 526.**

Dictionnaire Géographique, p. 1099.

Die Biblischen Sieben Jahre der Hungersnoth, 1891 (with facsimile of Inscription).

A History of Egypt under the Pharaohs, 1879, ii, p. 299.

BUDGE, E. A. W. *The Gods of the Egyptians*, i, p. 522.**

CATON, R. *The Harveian Oration*,[2] 1904.**

DARESSY, G. *Catalogue des Antiquités Égyptiennes du Musée du Caire : Statues de Divinités*, i. 17; ii. Pl. IV, V.**

ERMAN, A. *Handbook of Egyptian Religion*, pp. 76, 173.**

FOUCART, G. 'Imhotep.' *Revue de l'Histoire des Religions*, 1903, xlviii, p. 362.

GAUTHIER, H. 'Un Nouveau Monument du Dieu Imhotep.' *Bulletin de l'Institut Français d'Archéologie Orientale*, 1918, vol. xiv.

---

[1] Volumes marked with an * contain illustrations of Imhotep. Less important references are given in the notes appended to the text.

[2] Also published in the *Lancet*, 1904, i, p. 1769 ; *British Medical Journal*, 1904, i, p. 1473.

GRENFELL, B. P., and HUNT, A. S. *Oxyrhynchus Papyri*, 1915, Part XI, p. 221.

Lancet, The, 1915, ii, p. 1204.

JAYNE, W. A. *The Healing Gods of Ancient Civilisations*, 1925, p. 62.*

LANZONI, R. V. *Dizionario di Mitologia Egizia*, ii, p. 151, Pl. L.*

LEPSIUS, C. R. *Denkmäler aus Aegypten u. Äthiopien*, ix, Part IV, Pl. 15, 18, 19, 25.*

MASPERO, G. ' La IIIᵉ Dynastie Manéthonienne et le Dieu Imouthès.' *Études de Mythologie et d'Archéologie Égyptiennes*, 1916, viii, pp. 124 ff.

NAVILLE, E. *Temple of Deir el Bahari*, Part V, p. 11, Pl. CXLIX.*

PAULY, A. F. *Real-Encyclopädie der Classischen Altertumswissenschaft*, 1916, ix, col. 1213.

PIERRET, P. *Le Panthéon Égyptien*, 1881, pp. 77, 86, 101.*

ROSCHER, W. H. *Lexicon der Griechischen und Römischen Mythologie*, ii (i), p. 125.

SETHE, K. *Imhotep, der Asklepios der Aegypter. Untersuchungen zur Geschichte und Altertumskunde Aegyptens*, ii.

STRAUSS and TORNEY. *Entstehung und Geschichte des Altägyptischer Götterglaubes*, 1889, i, pp. 426–7.

WIEDEMANN, A. *Religion of the Ancient Egyptians*, 1897, p. 139.*

WILKINSON, J. G. *Manners and Customs of the Ancient Egyptians*, 1878, iii, p. 204.*

B. THE NAME IMHOTEP AND ITS
VARIANTS [1]

The name Imhotep may be spelt either 𓇋𓅓𓊵𓏏𓊪, 𓇋𓅓𓊵𓏏𓊪 or 𓇋𓅓𓊵 and may be transliterated Ij-m-ḥtp. The usually adopted modern vocalization is Imhotep, which the Greeks rendered as Ἰμούθης.

Personal names ending in the word *ḥtp* and compounded with the names of certain, but not with all, gods, were common in Egypt in all periods. Thus we find Rē-ḥotep, Ptaḥ-ḥotep, and similar compounds with the divine names Amen, Aah, Khons, Khnum, Mut, Min, Mont (Menthu), and others.[2] In these names the word ḥtp is the ' pseudo-participle ' or ' old perfective ' tense of the verb *ḥtp* ; the names therefore mean ' Re is satisfied ', ' Ptah is satisfied ', &c., and they are more correctly rendered—*Re-ḥotpe* or *Re-ḥotp*, &c. The verb *ḥtp* means to satisfy, and its use as a noun conveys the notion ' that which satisfies ', ' satisfier '. Its commonest use as a noun is with the meaning ' offerings ', as these, *par excellence*, in a primitive concept, are what bring satisfaction to a god. Its almost equally common significance ' peace ' is derived from the same series of ideas and refers to the state of the god's mind when due offerings have been made to him.

The name Imhotep, however, is quite differently constituted from the above God + ḥtp compounds. In this case ḥtp is a noun and means ' peace ' or ' satis-

---

[1] I am indebted to Mr. W. R. Dawson for some notes on the name Imhotep.

[2] Certain divine names are never found combined in this way, e. g. Osiris, Isis, Nephthys.

faction '. The translation ' he who comes in peace ' is the generally accepted one, although 𓇋 may be either the participle ' He who comes ' or the imperative ' Come '. The *em* or *m* can be either the preposition ' in ' or a particle meaning ' as ' or ' in guise of '. The name therefore means either ' one who comes in peace ' or ' a comer in peace '.[1]

VARIANTS IN THE SPELLING OF IMHOTEP

The Egyptian hieroglyphs, like most of the Semitic scripts, do not indicate vowels, nor indeed do they always accurately represent the consonantal skeleton. For these reasons there is no certainty how words were actually sounded, and a multiform transliteration, largely based on conjecture, has resulted. The following list of variants, which does not profess to be complete, will suffice to indicate the existing confusion and the urgency of some international agreement on the subject.[2]

Aiemapt   S. Birch, *Egypt from the Earliest Times to 300 B.C.*, p. 29.

Aiemhetp   Wilkinson, *Ancient Egyptians*, 1878, iii, p. 204.

[1] Names beginning with 𓇋 are not uncommon in the Old and Middle Kingdoms, e. g. 𓇋𓄿𓇋𓇋 I-MERY ' come, beloved ', 𓇋𓄪𓏏𓊭 I·M·SNB ' come in health '.

[2] Variants in which only small differences occur, such as the use of either the simple ' h ' or the guttural ' ḥ ', have not been included. Sethe discusses in detail the question of vocalization and accepts Imhotep as a satisfactory representation (Sethe, *Imhotep*, p. 1).

In the *Catalogue of the Demotic Papyri in the John Rylands Library*, iii, p. 437, F. Ll. Griffith gives the ways in which ' Imhotep ' was written in the time of Psammêtik I, Ahmasi II, Darius, and the early and late Ptolemies.

Aiemhotep	Wilkinson, *Ancient Egyptians*, 1878, iii, p. 204.
Ai-em-ḥetep	Budge, *An Egyptian Hieroglyphic Dictionary*, p. 30.
Aimhetep	Petrie, *A History of Egypt*, i, p. 30.
Eimhátpou	Maspero, *Études de Mythologie et d'Archéologie Égyptiennes*, 1916, viii, p. 124.
Ēm hō'tep	Breasted, *Ancient Times*, 1914, p. 737.
I-em-ḥetep	Budge, *Gods of the Ancient Egyptians*, i, p. 522.
I-em-hotep	Caton, *Harveian Oration*, 1904, p. 5.
Iemhotpe	Weigall, *History of the Pharaohs*, i, p. 6.
Iḥotep	Pauly, *Real-Encyclopädie*, ix, p. 1214.
Imhátpou	Maspero, *Études*, &c., viii, p. 124.
Im-ḥetep	Wiedemann, *Ägyptische Geschichte*, 1880, p. 220.
Imhoten	Wall, *Sex and Sex Worship*, p. 406.
Imhotep	*Encyclopaedia Britannica*, xxiv, p. 681.
Imhothès	*Revue de l'Histoire des Religions*, xlviii, p. 362.
Imhotp	*Encyclopaedia Britannica*, xiii, p. 245.
Imhotpe	*Encyclopaedia of Religion and Ethics*, xii, p. 780.
Imhotpou	Maspero, *Life in Ancient Egypt and Assyria*, p. 120.
Imhotpû	Maspero, *Dawn of Civilization*, p. 105.
Imhoutpé	Maspero, *Études de Mythologie et d'Archéologie Égyptiennes*, 1916, viii, p. 124.
Imhutep	Sethe, *Die Aegyptologie*, p. 7. (*Der Alte Orient*, 1923, xxiii.)
Imopth	*Records of the Past*, iv, p. 117.
Imothès	*Revue de l'Histoire des Religions*, xlviii, p. 367.
Imutep	Sethe, *Imhotep*, p. 12.
Iu-em-hept	A. B. Gosse, *Civilization of the Ancient Egyptians*, p. 112.

Yemhatpe   H. R. Hall, *The Observer*, Jan. 24, 1926.

Ŷmhetep   Lady Amherst, *A Sketch of Egyptian History*, p. 68.

Ymḥôtep   A. Erman, *Life in Ancient Egypt*, 1894, p. 386.

Ymhothphe H. R. Hall, *The Observer*, Jan. 24, 1926.

C. THE PEDIGREE OF IMHOTEP

In the Wadi Hammamat, the valley which runs down from Coptos to the Red Sea, the architect Khnum-ib-re (Chnem-eb-re), who between the years 495–491 B. C.[1] was occupied in quarrying stones for the Public Works Department, has left us an inscription which records the names of his ancestors, and in which Kanofer the father of Imhotep appears first and Imhotep holds the second place. The pedigree contains a list of twenty-five architects, all of whom are consecutively fathers and sons. Moreover, they are all master-builders.[2]

In this pedigree the earliest known ancestor is described as ' the chief of works, both of the South- and of of the North-land, governor of the capital and vizier, chief ritual priest of Zoser, the King of Upper and Lower Egypt, the son of Kanofer, chief of works of the South- and of the North-land '.

This master-builder, or chief of all the King's works, who was also chief ritual priest of King Zoser, must almost certainly have been Imhotep. The office of Master of the King's Works was evidently held in high honour, as was indeed the building industry in Egypt.

[1] i. e. from the 26th to the 30th year of the reign of Darius.

[2] Breasted uses the following expressions to indicate this office: ' master-builder ', ' chief of works ', ' leader of works ', ' master of works ', ' overseer of works '. Cf. his *Ancient Records of Egypt*, vol. v, Index V.

The following pedigree is reproduced from the list as given by Brugsch.[1]

THE PEDIGREE OF THE ARCHITECTS

KA NOFER : Architect of S. and N. Egypt.

IMHOTEP : Architect of S. and N. Egypt; chief burgomaster, a high functionary of King Z'a-sar (lived in the time of the IIIrd Dynasty).

R'A-HOTEP : Prophet of Amon-ra, king of the gods ; secret-seer of Heliopolis ; architect of Upper and Lower Egypt ; chief burgomaster.

BOK-EN-KHUNSU : Chief burgomaster.

UZA-KHUNSU : Architect ; chief burgomaster.

NOFER-MENNU : Architect : chief burgomaster.

MI (or AI ?) : Architect ; chief burgomaster.

SI-UER-NENEN-HIB : Architect.

PEPI : Architect ; chief burgomaster.

AMON-HIR-PI-MESH'A : 2nd, 3rd and 4th prophet and high-priest of Amon, king of the gods ; chief burgomaster.

HOR-EM-SAF : Chief burgomaster.

[1] H. Brugsch-Bey, *A History of Egypt under the Pharaohs*, 1879, ii, p. 299. In this list, in order to avoid confusion, Brugsch's spelling of the personal names is retained, even when it is inconsistent with that employed elsewhere in this volume.

MERMER :	Architect ; commander.
HOR-EM-SAF :	Architect ; commander.
ZA-HIB :	Architect ; commander.
NASSHUNU :	Architect ; commander.
ZA-HIB :	Architect ; commander.
NASSHUNU :	Architect ; commander.
ZA-HIB :	Architect ; commander.
NASSHUNU :	Architect ; commander.
ZA-N-HIBU :	Architect of Upper and Lower Egypt ; commander.
NASSHUNU :	Architect.
UAH-AB-R'A-RAN-UËR :	Architect.
'ANKH-PSAMTHIK :	Architect of Upper and Lower Egypt.
A'AHMES SI-NIT : (m. Sit-Nofer-tum)	Architect of Upper and Lower Egypt.
KHNUM-AB-R'A :	Chief minister of works for the whole country ; architect of Upper and Lower Egypt in the 27th to 30th years of King Darius I (about 490 B.C.).

D. STATUETTES OF IMHOTEP AS MEDICAL DEMIGOD

In most museums of Egyptology may be seen one or more bronze statuettes representing a somewhat diminutive dolichocephalic person who is evidently a learned scribe and who has on his knees an unrolled papyrus which he is reading attentively.[1]

These statuettes, usually from 12 to 20 cm. high, represent Imhotep as demigod, and belong to the Saite or Greek period.[2] The best of these statuettes are executed with unusual grace and delicacy, the face being well moulded and an excellent example of saitic art. Amongst the finest images are those at Cairo, the British Museum and the Wellcome Historical Medical Museum in London ; there are also excellent specimens at Paris, Berlin, Marseilles and Leiden. Many figures are enriched with gold, silver, and precious stones ; in other cases the inscriptions are inlaid with gold.

Although most of the statuettes are in solid bronze, some are made of glazed ware, steatite, imitation lapis-lazuli, electron, basalt or marble ;[3] at Cairo two specimens are of bronze with wooden seats (acacia and cedar). There are also amulet figures of glazed ware in London[4]

---

[1] A statuette in the Cairo Museum (No. 38063) shows a scribe's palette lying on the papyrus near the left hand. Cf. Daressy, *Statues de Divinités*, i.

[2] ' All the bronze figures of the god belong to a period subsequent to the XXIInd Dynasty.' E. A. Budge, *Gods of the Egyptians*, i, p. 525. According to Sethe (*Imhotep*, p. 1) these figures date from the period 700–332 B. C.

[3] A basalt statue 45 cm. high is preserved (*ca.* 660 B. C.) at the Louvre in the Salle des Monuments Religieux.

[4] At the Wellcome Historical Medical Museum.

and in Liverpool. The costume worn is usually that of a priest, a finely pleated apron hanging down over the knees and legs ; at other times the latter are bare. In one specimen at Cairo the legs are bandaged ;[1] occasionally there is nudity.[2] A closely fitted cap usually covers the head, although in other cases this is bald. A handsome necklace with four or more rows of beads is worn in many instances ; occasionally a pectoral is suspended by a cord. Although the sitting posture is usual, a few standing figures are known, where the roll of papyrus is held in the hand or under the arm. In rare cases the right hand grasps a pen, the left a roll of papyrus. In one instance a cynocephalus ape is held up.[3]

At the Cairo Museum of Antiquities are exhibited twenty-one statuettes, some of them of a highly artistic character. The British Museum possesses ten statuettes in a sitting posture. At the Wellcome Historical Medical Museum are thirty-three specimens, including two standing ones. The Ashmolean Museum at Oxford possesses three statuettes. At Berlin are three seated figures and one standing. The Metropolitan Museum of Art, New York, possesses six standing images and one sitting. The Louvre has about fifty specimens. Turin possesses five statuettes, four in bronze and one in blue glazed ware. At the Hermitage Museum, Petrograd, there are nine bronze images and one of glazed ware.

In many cases dedicatory inscriptions are added on the base, giving the name of the donor, who was probably

---

[1] G. Maspero, *The Dawn of Civilization*, p. 105.

[2] A. Erman, *Handbook of Egyptian Religion*, p. 174.

[3] As Imhotep was regarded as the god of learning he became associated with the animals sacred to Thoth, e. g. the ibis and cynocephalic ape. In later times he absorbed the duties of Thoth, as ' scribe of the gods '.

a sick person seeking health, or a grateful patient who had been cured. Thus the statuettes are votive in character.

The following is the inscription on one of the figures at Cairo, and gives the name of the donor followed by that of his father : ' Imhotep son of Ptah, born of Khreduonkh : Imhotep endowed with life ; Penek son of Uahibra.' Another inscription at Cairo (No. 38064) includes a specific prayer asking for ' great length of days and a great and happy old age '.

At the Wellcome Historical Medical Museum two figures bear the following inscriptions : ' Mes-son of Pedu-Ptah ' (Ptolemaic Period, *ca.* 300 B. C.) and ' Peteamensamtau '. At the British Museum, one figure is dedicated to Imhotep by Ptah-mes, and another by a devotee who is also called Imhotep. In the same collection is a figure of the god in the form of an ape reading a papyrus. This is probably a survival of animal worship, the ape being sacred to Thoth. At University College, London, is a figure dedicated by Wenamon son of Ta-Khred-Khons. At New York two open papyrus scrolls on the lap of the images have the following inscriptions : ' Imhotep, son of Ptah, born of Khreduonkh ' and ' Imhotep, son of the living Ptah '. One figure at Berlin (No. 2517) bears the inscription : ' Every scribe pours out to you a libation from his water bowl.' [1]

The form of seat occupied by sitting figures is usually plain ; in other cases elaborate mouldings are added, while in one of the finest examples at the Wellcome Historical Medical Museum the top of the seat is adorned with a row of about twenty uraei.

The human appearance of the figure represented in these statuettes is regarded by Erman as proving that

[1] *Königliche Museen zu Berlin, Ausführliches Verzeichniss der Aegyptischen Altertümer*, p. 299.

they belong to the period in which Imhotep was still regarded as a demigod and had not yet attained to the full status of deity.[1] These bronze figures form a striking contrast with his pictures dating from the Graeco-Roman period, when the deified man wears the costume and beard of a full deity, and holds the symbol of life in his hand.

E. MURAL FIGURES OF IMHOTEP AS DEITY

On the walls of various Egyptian and Nubian temples may be seen mural representations of the deity Imhotep carrying the uas sceptre and the ankh. In some cases the god is in a standing, in other cases in a sitting, posture. All these mural figures belong to the later Dynasties and correspond to the period of deification referred to above.

The figures are usually accompanied by inscriptions addressed to Imhotep. For instance, the inscription attached to the picture in the temple of Kasr el-Agouz referred to below reads thus : ' Son of Ptah, beneficent god, begotten by the god of the South Wall,[2] giver of life, who bestows gifts on those he loves, who listens [? to those who call upon him], who provides remedies for all diseases.' [3]

I. THEBES

(a) Karnak.

In the temple of Ptah and Hathor at Karnak, Imhotep with Ptah and his consort Hathor are seen sculptured on the walls and worshipped by King Tuthmosis III.

---

[1] A. Erman, *Aegypten*, ii, p. 477 ; Sethe, *Imhotep*, p. 4.
[2] i. e. Ptah.
[3] D. Mallet, *Le Kasr El-Agoûz*, 1909, p. 38.

Amenophis, the son of Hapi, was also worshipped in this temple.[1]

Ptolemy IV Philopator I, 222 B. C.

(b) Deir-el-Bahari.

In the temple of Hatshepsowet a standing figure of Imhotep is seen by the side of that of the deified sage Amenophis,[2] who was also regarded as a patron of healing.

Ptolemy IX Euergetes II, 147 B. C.

(c) Medinet Habu.

In this temple Imhotep is represented in company with several other gods of healing. Thus there is Thoth, a deity enjoying the reputation both of a magician and of a god of medicine. Another god of healing, named Teos, was also honoured. Lastly comes Amenophis. Imhotep, Amenophis, and Teos were all deified sages and appear as *paredroi* of Thoth, the Hermes of Egypt.[3]

(d) Deir el-Medineh.

In this small though graceful mortuary temple the deified Imhotep is again represented by the side of the deified sage Amenophis. The two figures may be seen

---

[1] A. E. Weigall, *Guide to the Antiquities of Upper Egypt*, 1913, p. 106. Cf. also G. Maspero, *Egypt, Ancient Sites and Modern Scenes*, p. 144 ; Lepsius, *Denkmäler*, ix, Part IV, Pl. 15 d. Imhotep appears only as a god with the Memphite deities, the Osiris group, and Amenophis, son of Hapi ; never with the Sun-deities. It will be observed that in most of the figures here described Amenophis appears as a sort of pendant to Imhotep. This association is somewhat surprising seeing the great dynastic interval between the two men. On the other hand, both were famous sages as well as architects and had filled the office of vizier to their respective kings. Cf. Piehl, *Z. f. Ägyptische Sprache*, 1887, xxv, p. 117.

[2] E. Naville, *Dêr el-Bahari*, Part V, p. 11 and Pl. CXLIX. Cf. also *J. of Egyptian Archaeology*, 1914, i, p. 96.

[3] Lepsius, *Denkmäler*, ix, Part IV, Pl. 32 c ; P. Boylan, *Thoth, the Hermes of Egypt*, 1922, pp. 166-8.

on two pillars with elaborate capitals just beyond the
first court.[1] This temple was begun by Ptolemy IV,
continued by Ptolemy VII, and finished by Ptolemy IX.
Hathor was regarded as its tutelary deity.

(*e*) Kasr el-Agouz.

In this temple, which was erected to the god Thoth and
is sometimes called after that deity, Imhotep is represented
as seated behind King Ptolemy Euergetes II and Thoth.
Imhotep is seen wearing a short shenti like that of Thoth,
while Amenophis the son of Hapi sitting behind Imhotep
is wearing the longer shenti of ceremony.[2]

Ptolemy IX Euergetes II, 116 B. C.

Brugsch (*Z. f. Ägyptische Sprache*, 1887, xxv, p. 117)
states that Imhotep with Amenophis as a sort of pendant
also appears on the wall of the temple of El-Assasif,
a short distance to the E. of the temple of Deir-el-Bahari.
The large-scale map of the Theban Necropolis, however,
published by the Survey Department, 1924, shows no
temple at Assasif.

II. PHILAE

On the Pylon of Imhotep's temple at Philae are five
figures of the god, three of which are standing and two
sitting. In one instance King Ptolemy V is offering
incense to the god ; in another the same king is offering
an image of the goddess Maat ; in a third he is offering
wine to Imhotep as well as to other deities. In the fourth
case the king is offering incense and libations, while in

[1] A. E. Weigall, *Guide to the Antiquities of Upper Egypt*,
1913, p. 277 ; Baedeker, *Egypt*, 1914, p. 317.
[2] D. Mallet, *Le Kasr El-Agoûz*, 1909, p. 38. Other reliefs
of Imhotep probably also existed in this temple. Cf. Mallet,
l. c., p. 35.

the last case he is seen grasping a club and standing in the presence of the god.[1]

At the entrance to the temple is another standing figure of the god Imhotep associated with Isis and Osiris and belonging to the same period.[2]

Ptolemy V Epiphanes, 205 B. C.

Lastly, in another part of the same temple at Philae the god is shown standing and associated with Isis and Harpocrates, all three being worshipped by eight cyno-cephalic apes.[3]

Ptolemy VII Philometer I, 173 B. C.

III. EDFU

A representation of Imhotep occurs on the inner west aspect of the surrounding wall of the temple of Edfu. He is wearing the leopard skin, as was usual for chief priests, and reading from a scroll the history of a civil war waged between the adherents of Horus and those of Set, which culminates in the two great defeats of the latter at Heliopolis and Ha or Hat.[4]

It is from the mythological fight between Horus and Set, in which Horus lost an eye, that is derived the sign which still figures at the head of our present-day medical prescriptions, viz. ℞, and which in its original form resembled a human eye.[5]

---

[1] Lepsius, *Denkmäler*, ix, Part IV, Pl. 18. Cf. also H. G. Lyons, *Report on the Island and Temples of Philae*, Pl. x ; A. E. Weigall, *Guide to the Antiquities of Upper Egypt*, 1913, p. 475. According to Sethe (*Imhotep*, p. 4), the mother of Imhotep, Khreduonkh, is seen with a human head and the hood of a vulture and double feathers.

[2] Lepsius, *Denkmäler*, ix, Part IV, Pl. 19.

[3] Lepsius, l. c., Pl. 25.

[4] A. E. Weigall, *A History of the Pharaohs*, i, p. 6.

[5] Cf. J. D. Comrie, *Edinburgh Med. J.*, 1909, ii, p. 119.

In this scene a priest called the *menhu* or slaughterer is seen cutting to pieces an animal which may be either a pig or a hippopotamus, representing Typhon (Set). Meanwhile Imhotep, the *Kheri-heb*, clad in a leopard's skin and wearing a sort of helmet reads the justification of Horus. Close by is the following inscription :

' Chief priest, scribe of the god, Imhotep, the great one, son of Ptah.'

Naville thus refers to the scene : [1] ' This priest, *Imhotep uer si Ptah*, interests us particularly, not because he is invested with one of the chief sacerdotal posts in the temple of Edfou, but because he was also its architect ; at least he directed the construction of certain parts of the edifice. This is the only monument where we find the signature of the artist who made its plan.'

Imhotep proclaims Horus justified in the *usecht*, i.e. in one of the great halls of the temple.

IV. NUBIA

(*a*) Débôt.

In this temple Imhotep is represented three times, once in the temple itself, and twice in the chapel of the Nubian king Azkheramon.[2]

Weigall thus describes one of the scenes :

' As one enters the roofless pronaos the reliefs on the inner sides of the doorway are seen to represent Horus and Thoth pouring a vessel of holy water over the approaching worshipper, while behind them " the Chief

[1] E. Naville, *Textes relatifs au Mythe d'Horus, recueillis dans le temple d'Edfou*, 1870, p. 15, Pl. XI.

[2] G. Roeder, *Les Temples immergés de la Nubie*, 1911, i, pp. 47, 52, 53 ; ii, Pls. 12, 13, 44.

Reader-priest, the Chief Scribe of the North and South ",
the demigod Imhotep, sees that the necessary ritual is
said.' [1]

(*b*) Dakkah.
Here there are two scenes in which Imhotep appears.[2]
? Ptolemy IX Euergetes II.

(*c*) Kalabshah.
Imhotep is here represented as receiving a gift of
incense from the Emperor Augustus.[3]
? Ptolemaic Period.

(*d*) Meroë.
It is possible that a relief in one of the pyramids of
Meroë (No. 12) is intended to represent Imhotep, but no
positive assertion can be made on the subject. The
reliefs in the chapel concerned are reproduced by Lepsius,[4] and the drawing in question shows a figure similar
to that of the deified Imhotep, but without ankh, and
only holding an ordinary staff instead of the uas sceptre.
Budge describes the scene as that of ' The deceased
adoring an ancestor (or I-em-ḥetep) '.[5]

---

[1] A. E. Weigall, *Guide to the Antiquities of Upper Egypt*,
1913, p, 492 ; *Antiquities of Lower Nubia*, 1907, p. 58.
[2] *Bulletin de l'Institut Français d'Archéologie Orientale*,
1918, xiv, Fasc. I, p. 40.
[3] H. Gauthier, *Les Temples immergés de la Nubie*, 1911, i,
p. 88, Pl. xxvii b. Imhotep is wearing a uraeus and is carrying
a sceptre and an ankh.
[4] Lepsius, *Denkmäler*, x, Part V, Pl. 26.
[5] E. A. Budge, *The Egyptian Sudan*, i, p. 400.

INDEX

(PERSONS, PLACES AND SUBJECTS)

SBN –19–	Author	Title
443567	ALFÖLDI A.	The Conversion of Constantine and Pagan Rome
241775	ALLEN T.W	Homeri Ilias (3 volumes)
286409	ANDERSON George K.	The Literature of the Anglo-Saxons
219601	ARNOLD Benjamin	German Knighthood
208618	ARNOLD T.W.	The Caliphate
228813	BARTLETT & MacKAY	Medieval Frontier Societies
219733	BARTLETT Robert	Trial by Fire and Water
11010	BETHURUM Dorothy	Homilies of Wulfstan
142765	BOLLING G. M.	External Evidence for Interpolation in Homer
14332X	BOLTON J.D.P.	Aristeas of Proconnesus
240132	BOYLAN Patrick	Thoth, the Hermes of Egypt
14222	BROOKS Kenneth R.	Andreas and the Fates of the Apostles
14715	BUCKLER Georgina	Anna Comnena
03543	BULL Marcus	Knightly Piety & Lay Response to the First Crusade
16785	BUTLER Alfred J.	Arab Conquest of Egypt
48046	CAMERON Alan	Circus Factions
48054	CAMERON Alan	Porphyrius the Charioteer
48348	CAMPBELL J.B.	The Emperor and the Roman Army 31 BC to 235
6643X	CHADWICK Henry	Priscillian of Avila
6447X	CHADWICK Henry	Boethius
22025	COLGRAVE B. & MYNORS R.A.B.	Bede's Ecclesiastical History of the English People
31658	COOK J.M.	The Troad
19393	COWDREY H.E.J.	The Age of Abbot Desiderius
44043	CRUM W.E.	Coptic Dictionary
8992	DAVIES M.	Sophocles: Trachiniae
5301X	DOWNER L.	Leges Henrici Primi
346X	DRONKE Peter	Medieval Latin and the Rise of European Love-Lyric
2749	DUNBABIN T.J.	The Western Greeks
4372	FAULKNER R.O.	The Ancient Egyptian Pyramid Texts
1541	FLANAGAN Marie Therese	Irish Society, Anglo-Norman Settlers, Angevin Kingship
3109	FRAENKEL Edward	Horace
1540	GOLDBERG P.J.P.	Women, Work and Life Cycle in a Medieval Economy
0215	GOTTSCHALK H.B.	Heraclides of Pontus
6162	HANSON R.P.C.	Saint Patrick
4354	HARRISS G.L.	King, Parliament and Public Finance in Medieval England to 1369
1114	HEATH Sir Thomas	Aristarchus of Samos
0444	HOLLIS A.S.	Callimachus: Hecale
2968	HOLLISTER C. Warren	Anglo-Saxon Military Institutions
5470	HOULDING J.A.	Fit for Service
5480	HENRY Blanche	British Botanical and Horticultural Literature before 1800
0523	HOUSLEY Norman	The Italian Crusades
3129	HURNARD Naomi	The King's Pardon for Homicide – before AD 1307
1783	HURRY Jamieson B.	Imhotep
0401	HUTCHINSON G.O.	Hellenistic Poetry
0140	JOACHIM H.H.	Aristotle: On Coming-to-be and Passing-away
0094	JONES A.H.M	Cities of the Eastern Roman Provinces
560	JONES A.H.M.	The Greek City
354	JONES Michael	Ducal Brittany 1364–1399
484	KNOX & PELCZYNSKI	Hegel's Political Writings
755	LAWRENCE C.H.	St Edmund of Abingdon
253	LE PATOUREL John	The Norman Empire
720	LENNARD Reginald	Rural England 1086–1135
321	LEVISON W.	England and the Continent in the 8th century
224	LIEBESCHUETZ J.H.W.G.	Continuity and Change in Roman Religion
486	LINDSAY W.M.	Early Latin Verse
378	LOBEL Edgar & PAGE Sir Denys	Poetarum Lesbiorum Fragmenta
159	LOEW E.A.	The Beneventan Script
445	LUKASIEWICZ, Jan	Aristotle's Syllogistic
442	MAAS P. & TRYPANIS C.A .	Sancti Romani Melodi Cantica
584	MARSDEN E.W.	Greek and Roman Artillery—Historical
592	MARSDEN E.W.	Greek and Roman Artillery—Technical
178	MATTHEWS John	Western Aristocracies and Imperial Court AD 364–425
205	MAVROGORDATO John	Digenes Akrites
47	McFARLANE K.B.	Lancastrian Kings and Lollard Knights
578	McFARLANE K.B.	The Nobility of Later Medieval England
6X	MEIGGS Russell	The Athenian Empire
00	MEIGGS Russell	Roman Ostia
02	MEIGGS Russell	Trees and Timber in the Ancient Mediterranean World